I SURVIVED 203 STEPS

Some of America's Tallest Lighthouses 150 Feet and Taller

Richard E. Tubbs

ISBN: 979-8-9872203-6-8 (Paperback)
ISBN: 979-8-9872203-8-2 (Hardcover)
eISBN: 979-8-9872203-7-5

DEDICATION

I dedicate this book to my wife, best friend and fellow lighthouse lover,
Linda Chip Carol Tubbs, I love you!

TABLE OF CONTENTS

INTRODUCTION

Lighthouses!? Again?! This is more than just another lighthouse photo book. It is more than another inspirational book. It is a collection of awesome photos that have some inspiring scripture on them with some cool stats for each lighthouse. And, I encourage you to cut out any and all of the photos you like and hang them by any means you have – think tape, tacks, pins, frames, etc. This will allow you to see an amazing photo often and an inspiring word of encouragement when needed.

The lighthouses are all 150 feet and taller that I have visited. They are arranged in descending order from Cape Hatteras Lighthouse at 208 feet tall down to Pensacola Lighthouse at 150 feet tall. I have climbed almost all of these lighthouses. You can't climb them if they are closed, being renovated or it is outside of normal visiting hours.

An interesting subject is how tall a lighthouse is. Some lighthouses are reported at different heights. Since a lighthouse is a building, they are supposed to be measured from the top of the foundation or the part of the building that is at ground level to the highest point, which may be a roof peak, a chimney, a spire, an antenna, a knob etc. Some people want to measure a lighthouse including it's foundation, or even how many feet above sea level the ground the lighthouse is on, and some want to exclude the base. A lighthouse is properly measured from the ground it is on top of to the very highest point – a spike or knob or roof peak. All of the heights I am using are this last measurement description.

A more complex subject is a lighthouse's focal plane. A Focal Plane is how far away an object can be seen. We are talking about how far away the lighthouses light can be seen, specifically out to sea. Easier to describe than tell how to calculate. It is measured along the idea of measuring a triangle's sides. You start at how tall an object is or how far off the ground it is. In this case, a lighthouse's lantern – the light itself, not the highest point. Most lights are around 4 to 6 feet lower than the tallest point of a lighthouse. And most distances calculated assume that the one looking for the light is on a vessel and is 15 feet above sea level, or above the water. You then apply a formula. A mathematician did a formula, out here: https://www.mathscinotes.com/2015/04/lighthouse-visual-ranges/, that does give the same distances that the Coast Guard says a light can be seen at. The Coast Guard has a nice table, out here: https://www.navcen.uscg.gov/pdf/lightLists/LightList_V3_2022.pdf on the Luminous Range Diagram page. Bummer, the Coast Guard does not give the formula they use, nor does the previous lighthouse organizations. And the National Park Service (NPS) also gives a warning or disclaimer that it also depends on the size of your boat, the weather and the tower's height, https://www.uscg.mil/Portals/0/OurOrganization/auxiliary/publications/auxmanuals/ATON2000StudyGuideSec2ATON.pdf?ver=2017-07-02-093515-290.

And the last subject we need to discuss, in regards to facts, in this book, are steps. There is no standard for the size of a step. No required height, depth or width. So, the lighthouse architects designed the step sizes based off their own desire or whim. To illustrate this, I'll use Ponce de Leon Inlet and St Augustine, both designed off of Cape Hatteras' design. Ponce Inlet is 175 feet tall with 203 steps and St Augustine is 165 feet tall with 219 steps. No step is the same. It is more exercise to climb the 219 steps than the 203. But both of them can be exhausting. You will find the steps are not so bad to climb, by stopping at the windows and landings that are built into the lighthouses' staircases.

I have gathered data for each lighthouse from various sources on purpose. This allowed me to verify the data. I do recommend that you do the same, if you find any data that I present as different than the data you use for any lighthouse. This is how I discovered the various height discrepancies. Measuring from the ground up to the light itself, the focal plane, is not the correct height. And that not all steps are created equal, just like not all people's builds are created equal.

So, go enjoy the book! Debate the facts with sources to back up your facts. And don't hesitate to hang the photos where you can use the great pictures and inspiring quotes.

CAPE HATTERAS
LIGHTHOUSE

CAPE HATTERAS LIGHTHOUSE, Outer Banks, Buxton, North Carolina

Stood 208 feet tall at the old site and 210.01 feet at the new site. (1) Others list it at 207 feet or 210 feet, etc. National Park Service (NPS) measures it at 198.49 feet tall. (2)

There are 269 steps. (3) Only 257 steps do visitors climb (4), to a height of 166 feet.

Built in 1870.

Moved in 1999, 2,900 feet to its current site. The old site is being taken back by the ocean.

The U.S. National Park Service operates and does upkeep on the grounds, tower and other buildings. US Coast Guard operates and maintains the automated light.

Open to the Public year-round.

Tower is open for climbing and self-guided tours from the third Friday in April to Columbus Day in October.

Originally a Fresnel Lens, 1st Order, the largest size, 12 feet tall and about 2,500 pounds of glass and bronze. The lens was removed in 1949 and now it is in the Graveyard of the Atlantic Museum, 10 miles away in Hatteras Village.

1st electrified in 1934. The present day beacon is electric, upgraded in 1982. It is two 1000-watt lamps with 800,000-candlepower rotary beacon, that flashes two beams every 7.5 seconds. No Fresnel Lens is needed as these lights use two parabolic reflectors.

Focal plane, how far out to sea it can be seen, is between 15.6 and 24 nautical miles,(5) depending on the size of your boat.

The towers height and air clarity, also, determines how far out to sea it can be seen on any given night.(6)

Location: On Cape Hatteras National Seashore, near Cape Hatteras, in Buxton, North Carolina. (7)

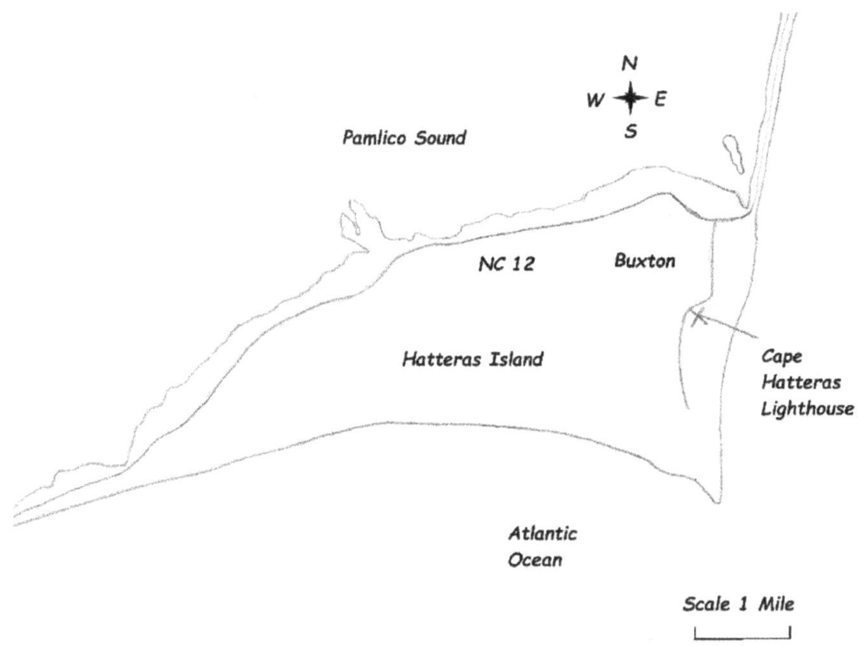

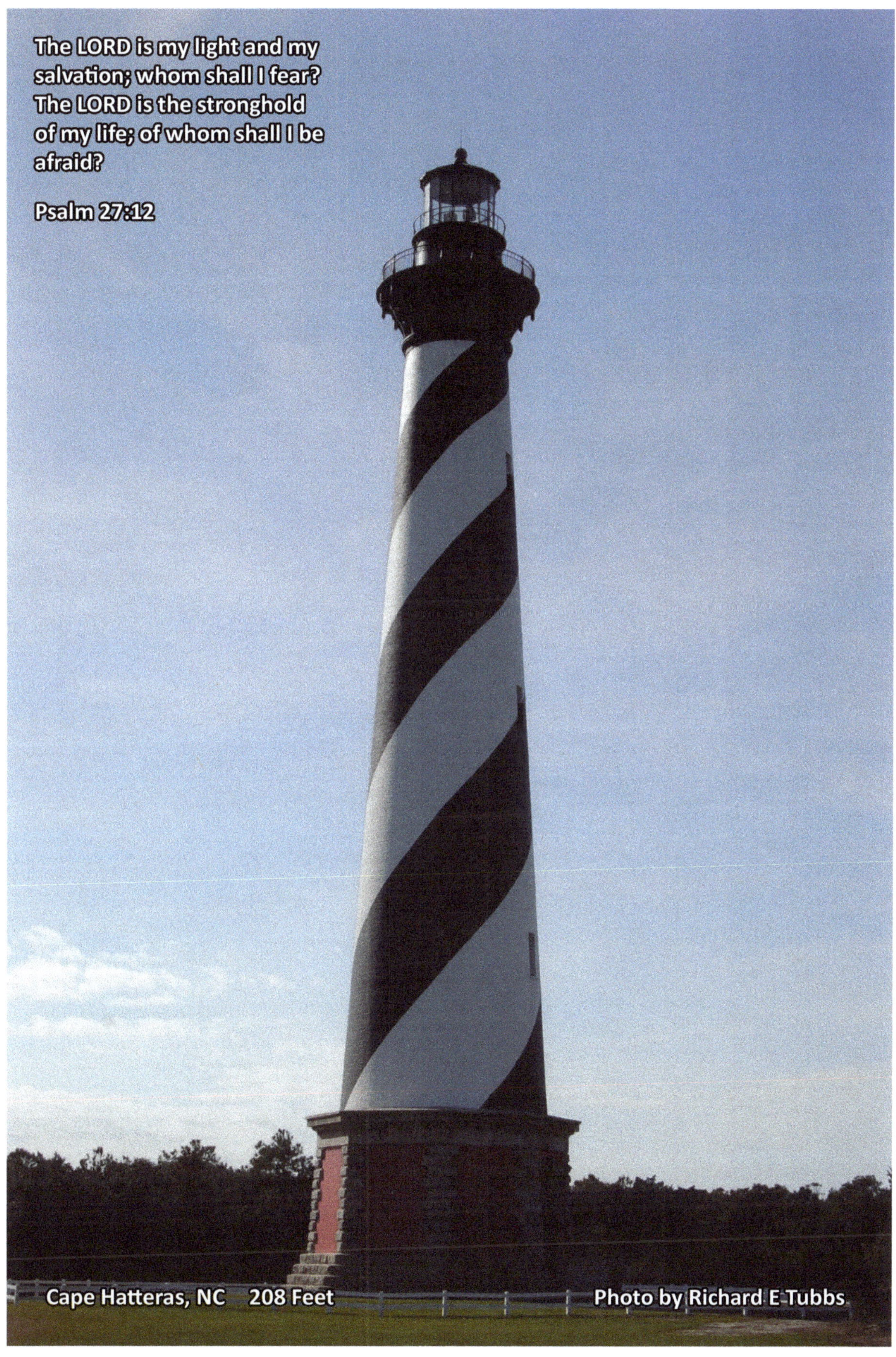
The LORD is my light and my salvation; whom shall I fear? The LORD is the stronghold of my life; of whom shall I be afraid?

Psalm 27:12

Cape Hatteras, NC   208 Feet
Photo by Richard E Tubbs

PONCE DE LEON INLET LIGHTHOUSE

PONCE DE LEON INLET LIGHTHOUSE, Ponce Inlet, Florida

Ponce de Leon Inlet Lighthouse Preservation Association, who owns it and operates it, measures it at 175 feet tall.

There are 203 steps.

Built in 1887.

Originally named the Mosquito Inlet Lightstation. Name changed to Ponce de Leon Inlet Lighthouse in 1927.

Open to the Public year-round.

Tower is open for climbing and self-guided tours. The Keepers Dwellings, 10 of the out buildings and grounds are museums.(1)

Ponce Inlet uses a 3rd Order Fresnel Lens, the 3rd largest size, 12 feet tall and about 2,000 pounds of glass and bronze. (2)

The Light was converted to electric in 1933. This light rotated producing six flashes in a fifteen-second period followed by a fifteen-second eclipse. Completely automated in 1953. In 1996 lightning struck the tower and the light was upgraded to a 500 watt electric lamp, 220,000 candlepower, Vega VBR-25 Marine Rotating Beacon, with a flash every 10 seconds.

Original 1st Order Fresnel Lens has been restored and is on display, on site, in the Ayres Davies Lens Exhibit Building.

Focal plane, how far out to sea it can be seen, is between 18 and 20 nautical miles (3), depending on the size of your boat.

The towers height and air clarity, also, determines how far out to sea it can be seen on any given night. (4)

Location: On Ponce Inlet, Florida. (5)

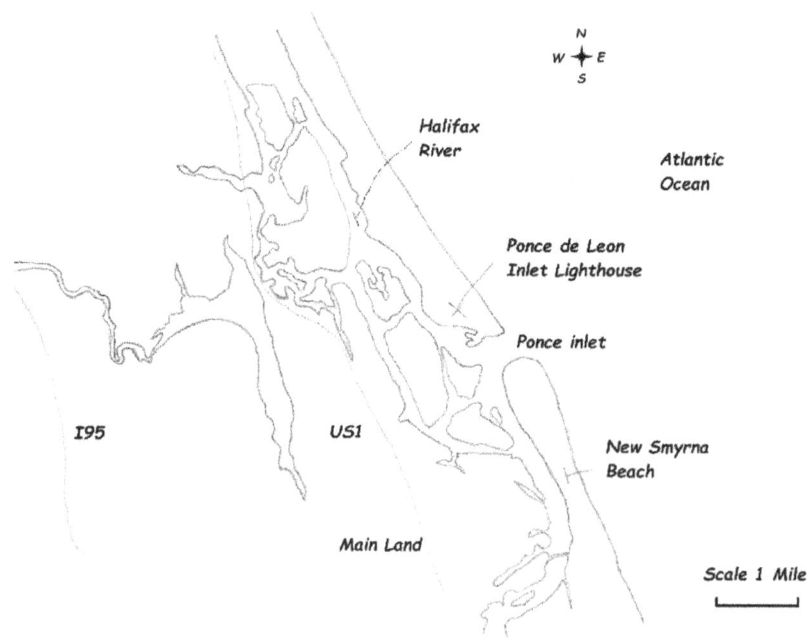

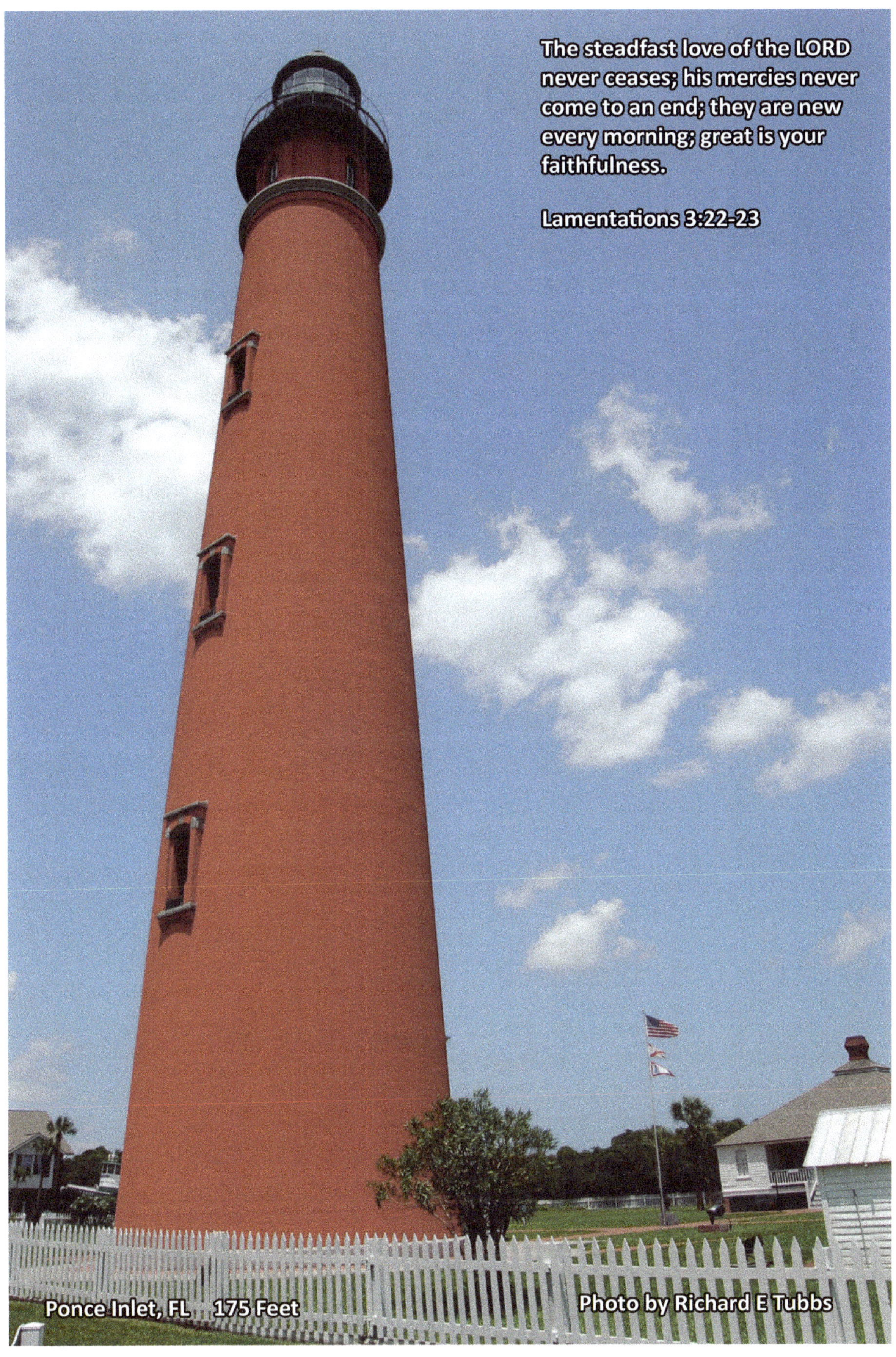
The steadfast love of the LORD
never ceases; his mercies never
come to an end; they are new
every morning; great is your
faithfulness.

Lamentations 3:22-23

Ponce Inlet, FL   175 Feet

Photo by Richard E Tubbs

ST AUGUSTINE LIGHTHOUSE

ST AUGUSTINE LIGHTHOUSE, St. Augustine, Florida

Stands 165 feet tall.(1)

There are 219 steps.

Built in 1874.

Operated by the St. Augustine Lighthouse & Maritime Museum.

Open to the Public year-round (closed on Thanksgiving and Christmas). Tower is open for climbing and self-guided tours. The Keepers Dwellings, some out buildings and grounds are museums.

Uses a Sauter and Lemonier First Order Fresnel Lens, 9 feet tall, three fixed flashes from three bulls-eye panels every three minutes. In 1936 changed to 30 second flash. (2) About 2 tons of glass and steel. (https://www.staugustinelighthouse.org/get-involved/about-mission-uvp/history/)

The light was converted to electric in 1936. Automated in 1971. Uses a 1000 watt bulb. (3)

Focal plane, how far out to sea it can be seen, is 19 to 24 nautical miles, (4) depending on the size of your boat.

The towers height and air clarity also determines how far out to sea it can be seen on any given night. (5)

Location: On ANASTASIA ISLAND, St. Augustine, Florida. (6)

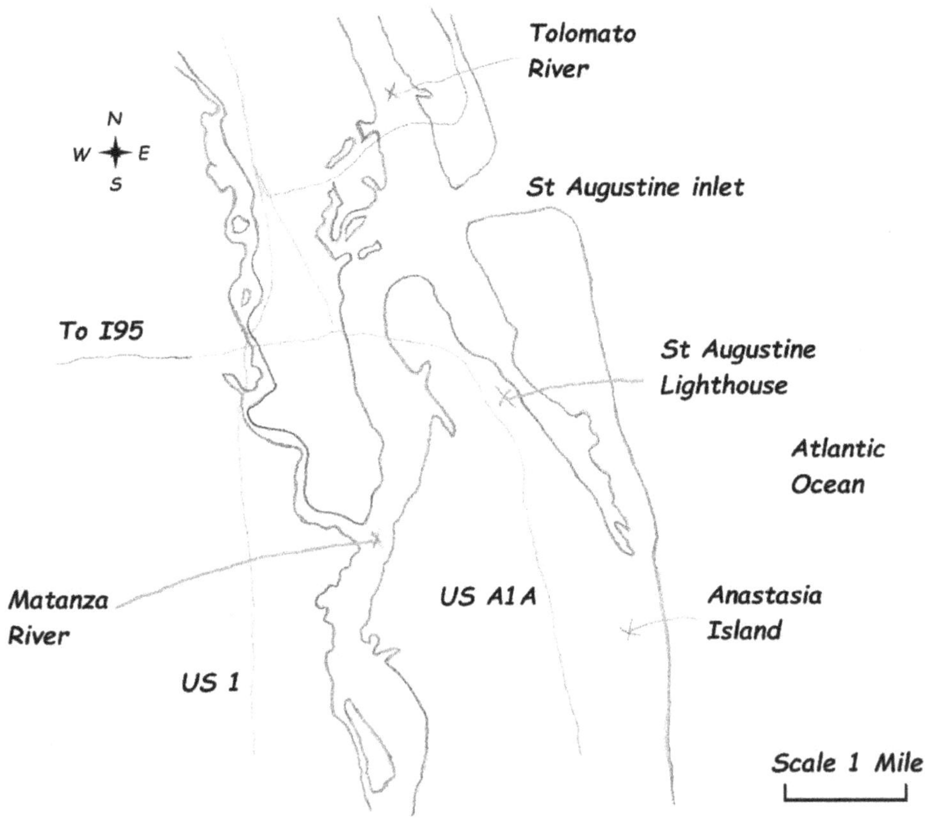

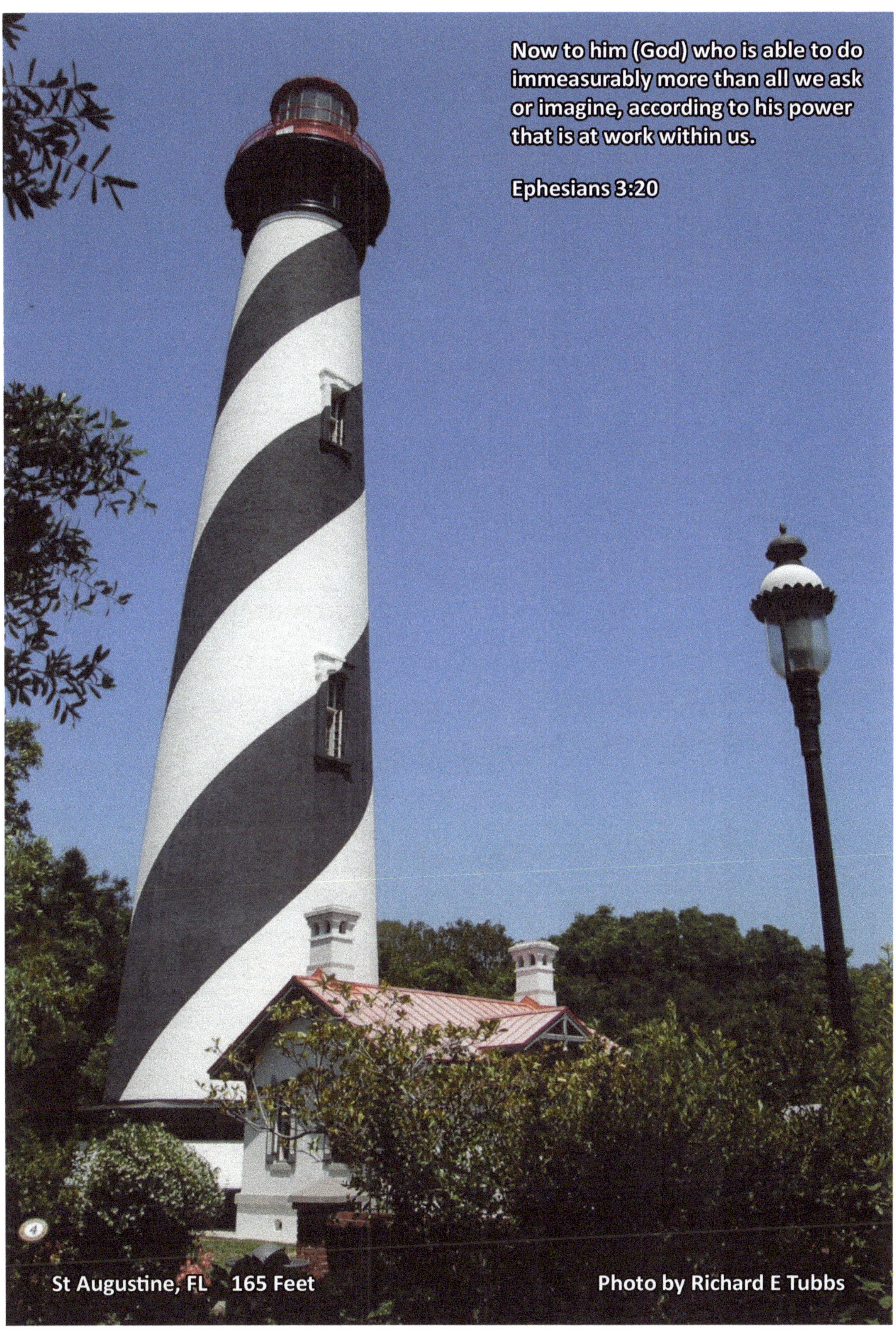
Now to him (God) who is able to do immeasurably more than all we ask or imagine, according to his power that is at work within us.

Ephesians 3:20

St Augustine, FL   165 Feet

Photo by Richard E Tubbs

CAPE LOOKOUT
LIGHTHOUSE

CAPE LOOKOUT LIGHTHOUSE,
Outer Banks, Harkers Island, North Carolina

Stands 163 feet tall.

There are 207 steps.

Built in 1859.

Operated by the U.S. National Park Service. (1) Light is maintained by the United States Coast Guard. (2)

The Cape Lookout National Seashore is open to the Public 24/7 year-round. Lighthouse is closed for climbing due to structural repairs that are expected to be completed for the 2025 climbing season, per NPS.

Originally had a 1st Order Fresnel Lens, the largest size, 12 feet tall and about 2,500 pounds of glass and bronze.

In 1933, electric lamps were installed. Original light had no flash, it was constantly on. In 1914, it went to 3 9 second flashes, then, 1 9 second flash twice every 90 seconds. In 1933, the flash was changed to on for 2 seconds off for 2 seconds on for 2 seconds and off for 9 seconds. The light was automated in 1950. Today, it flashes once every 15 seconds. (3) In 2017, the lighthouse was solarized and the beacons were replaced with a multi-tier LED optic, 80,000 candle power. (4)

Focal plane, how far out to sea it can be seen, is 19 nautical miles, (5) depending on the size of your boat. The towers height and air clarity, also, determines how far out to sea it can be seen on any given night. (6)

Location: On Core Banks (of the Outer Banks) in the Cape Lookout National Seashore, North Carolina. (7)

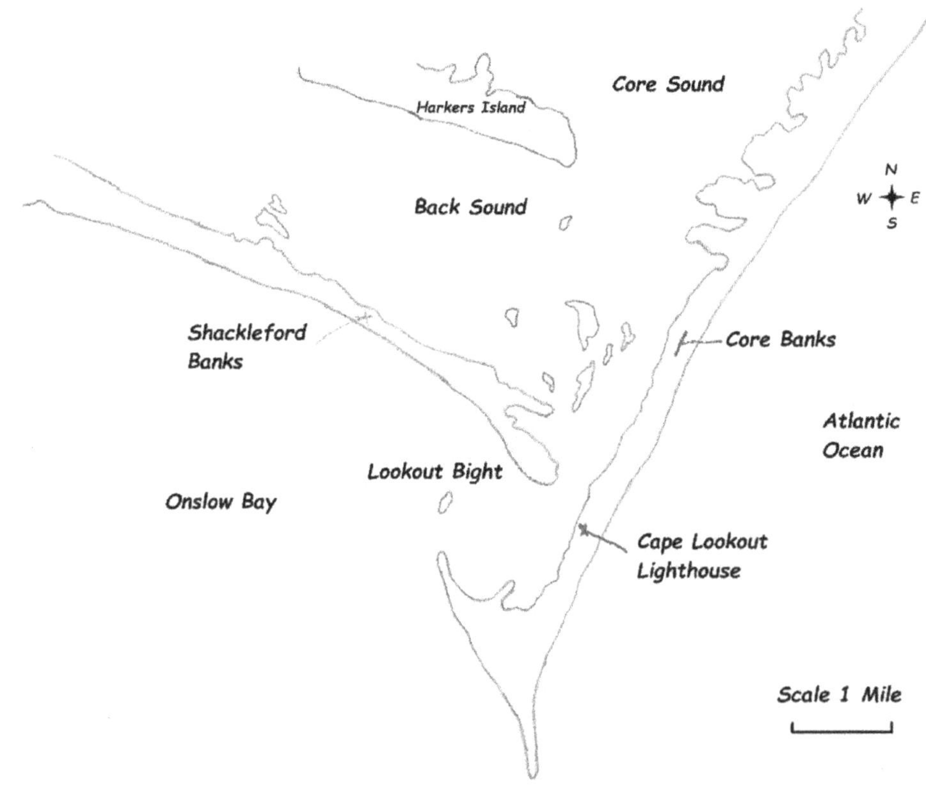

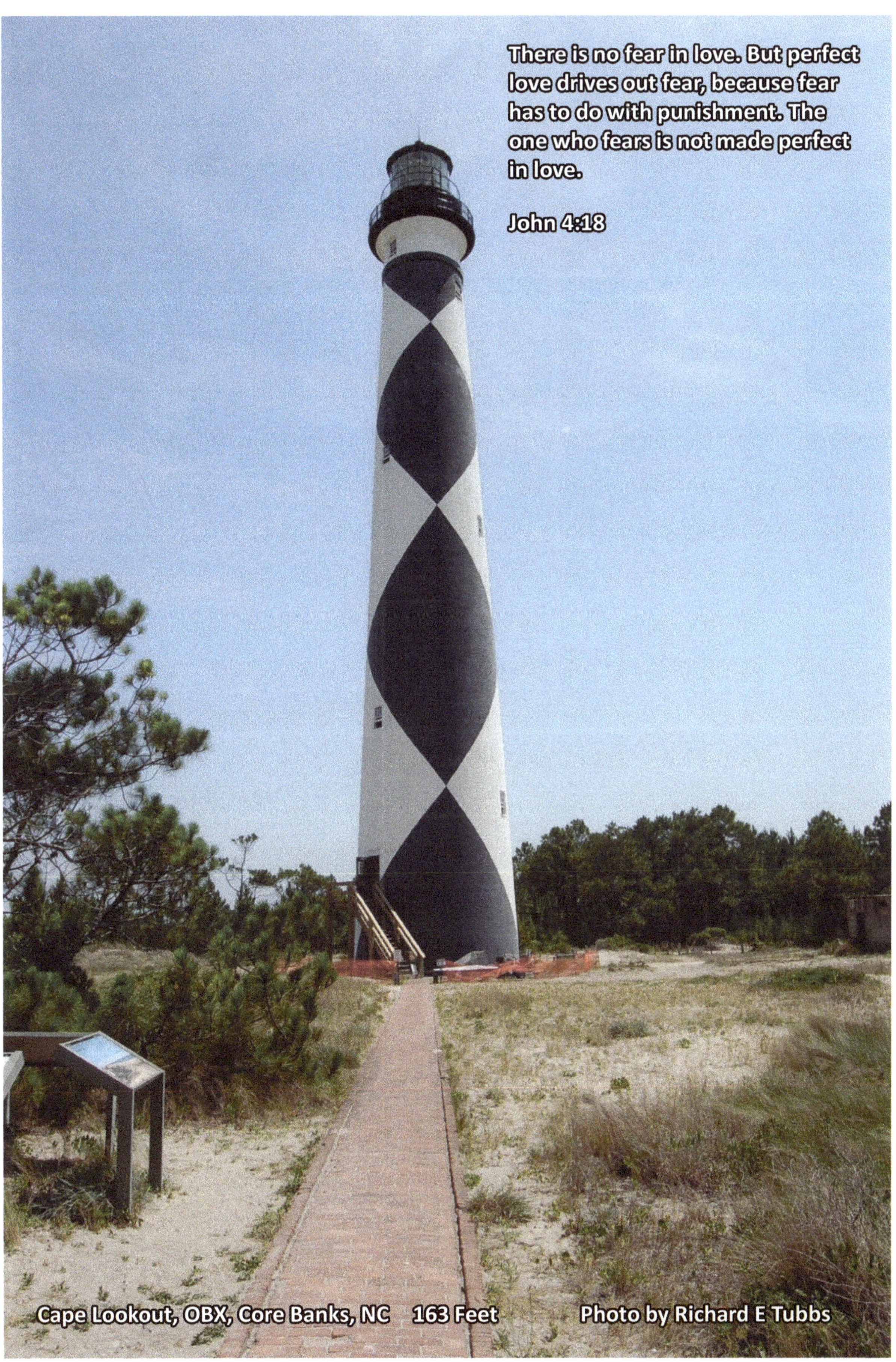
There is no fear in love. But perfect love drives out fear, because fear has to do with punishment. The one who fears is not made perfect in love.

John 4:18

Cape Lookout, OBX, Core Banks, NC   163 Feet   Photo by Richard E Tubbs

CURRITUCK BEACH LIGHTHOUSE

CURRITUCK BEACH LIGHTHOUSE, Corolla, North Carolina

Stands 162 feet tall.

There are 220 steps.

Built in 1875.

Operated by the Outer Banks Conservationists (OBC), Inc. Open to the Public. Grounds are open year-round. Lighthouse and Museum Shop are open mid-March to December. You can climb the tower and take a self-guided tour. The Keepers Dwellings and grounds are museums.

It has a First Order Fresnel Lens, 12 feet tall, 20 second flash white light (1) with a red flash every ninety-seconds. About 2 tons of glass and steel. (2)

The light was converted to electric in 1933 and automated in 1937.

Focal plane, how far out to sea it can be seen, is 18 nautical miles, (3) depending on the size of your boat. The towers height and air clarity also determines how far out to sea it can be seen on any given night. (4)

Location: On the Northern Most tip of the Outer Banks, Corolla, North Carolina. (5)

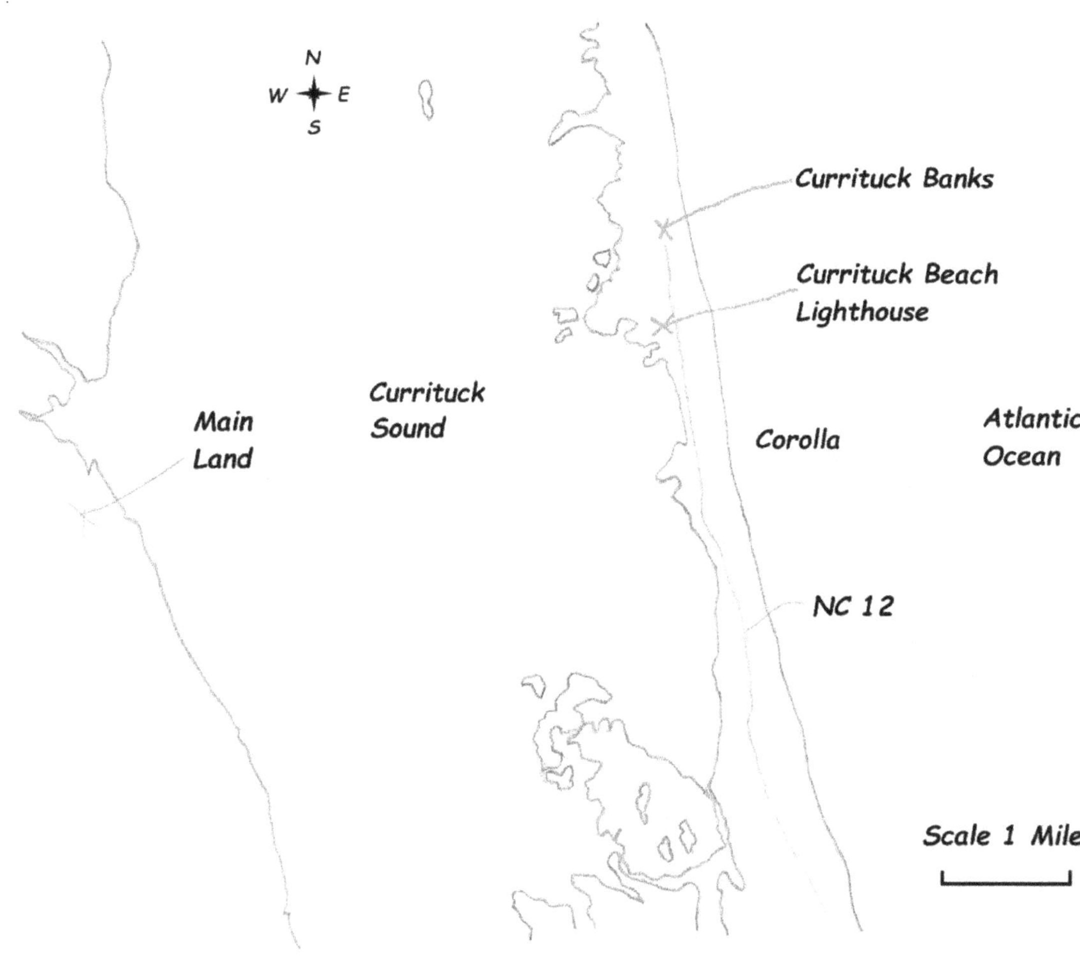

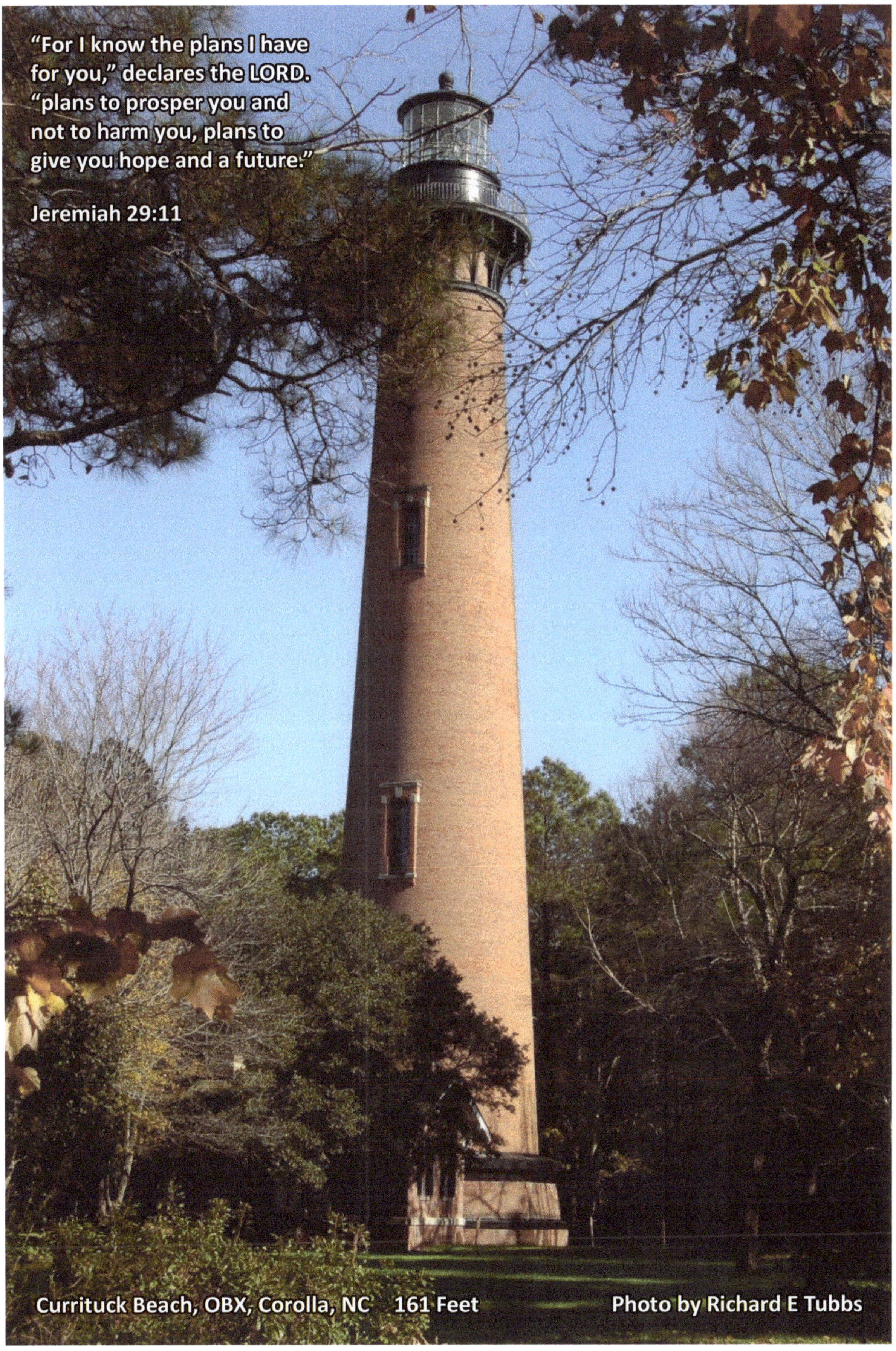
"For I know the plans I have
for you," declares the LORD.
"plans to prosper you and
not to harm you, plans to
give you hope and a future."

Jeremiah 29:11

Currituck Beach, OBX, Corolla, NC   161 Feet   Photo by Richard E Tubbs

MORRIS ISLAND LIGHTHOUSE

MORRIS ISLAND LIGHTHOUSE, Morris Island, South Carolina

Stands 161 feet tall.

There are 201 steps. (1)

Built in 1876.

Operated by the State of South Carolina and maintained by Save The Light, Inc. Closed to the public.

Stands a few hundred feet off the coast, at the north end of Folly Beach on Morris Island in the Charleston Harbor. (2)

Originally had a 1st Order Fresnel Lens, the largest size, 12 feet tall and about 2 tons of glass, steel and bronze. Light was converted to electric in 1938 and first order Fresnel lens was removed and is on display at the Hunting Island Lighthouse.

Focal plane, how far out to sea it could be seen, is 18.75 nautical miles (3) depending on the size of your boat.(4) In 1962, the state officials deemed the light too close to shore and had it closed down. The light was extinguished for regular navigational use. (5) Since then, lit by the Save The Light for celebrations etc. (6) The towers height and air clarity also determines how far out to sea it can be seen on any given night. (7)

Location: Just north of Folly Beach, off shore over 1,600 feet away, at the entrance to Charleston Harbor on Morris Island, South Carolina. (8)

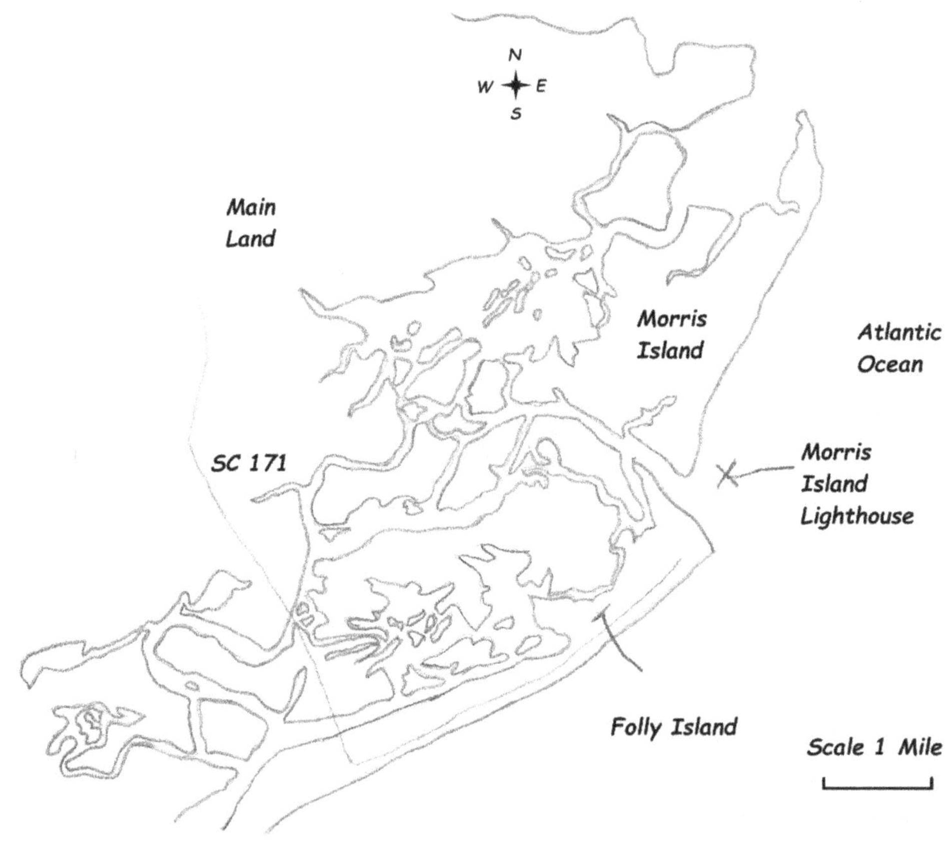

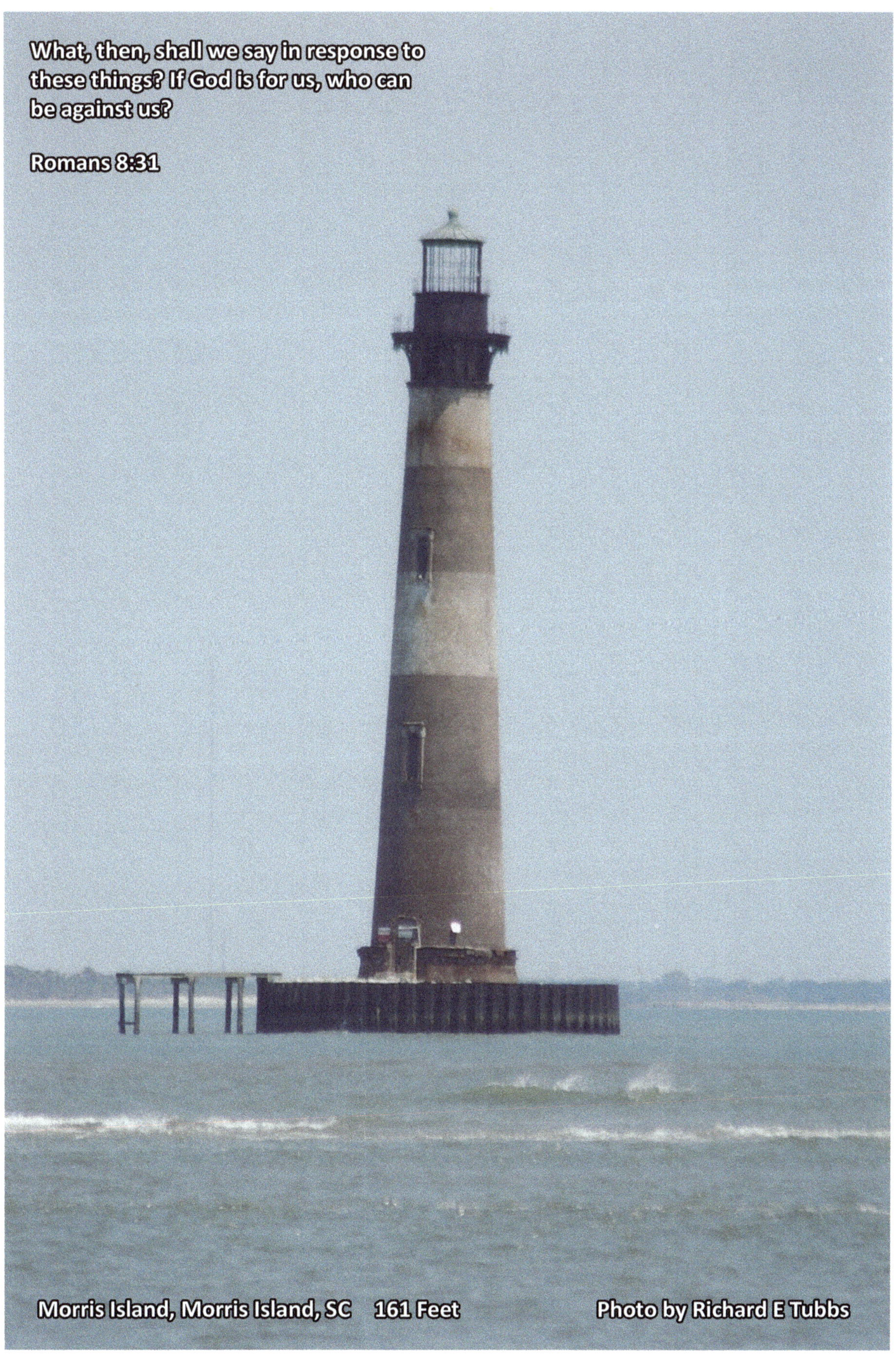
What, then, shall we say in response to
these things? If God is for us, who can
be against us?

Romans 8:31

Morris Island, Morris Island, SC   161 Feet   Photo by Richard E Tubbs

BODIE (Body) ISLAND LIGHTHOUSE

BODIE (Body) ISLAND LIGHTHOUSE, Nags Head, North Carolina

Bodie Island Lighthouse is pronounced like the word "Body." It does not have a long "OH" sound. (1)

Stands 158 feet tall according to NPS. (2) Or 156 feet per Outer Banks website, outerbanks.com. (https://www.outerbanks.com/bodie-island-lighthouse.html)

There are 214 steps. (3)

Built in 1872.

Operated and maintained by the National Parks Service. Open to the public for self-guided climbs from the third Friday in April to Columbus Day in October. Grounds are open year-round. (4)

Uses a 1st Order Fresnel Lens, the largest size, 12 feet tall and about 2 tons of glass, steel and bronze.

The light was converted to electric in 1932. And fully automated in 1940.

Focal plane, how far out to sea it can be seen, is 18.75 nautical miles (5), depending on the size of your boat. The towers height and air clarity also determines how far out to sea it can be seen on any given night. (6)

Location: Just south of Nags Head, and is approximately 7 miles south of Whalebone Junction, which is the intersection of US 64, US 158, and NC Highway 12, the northern end of Cape Hatteras National Seashore, OBX, NC. (7)

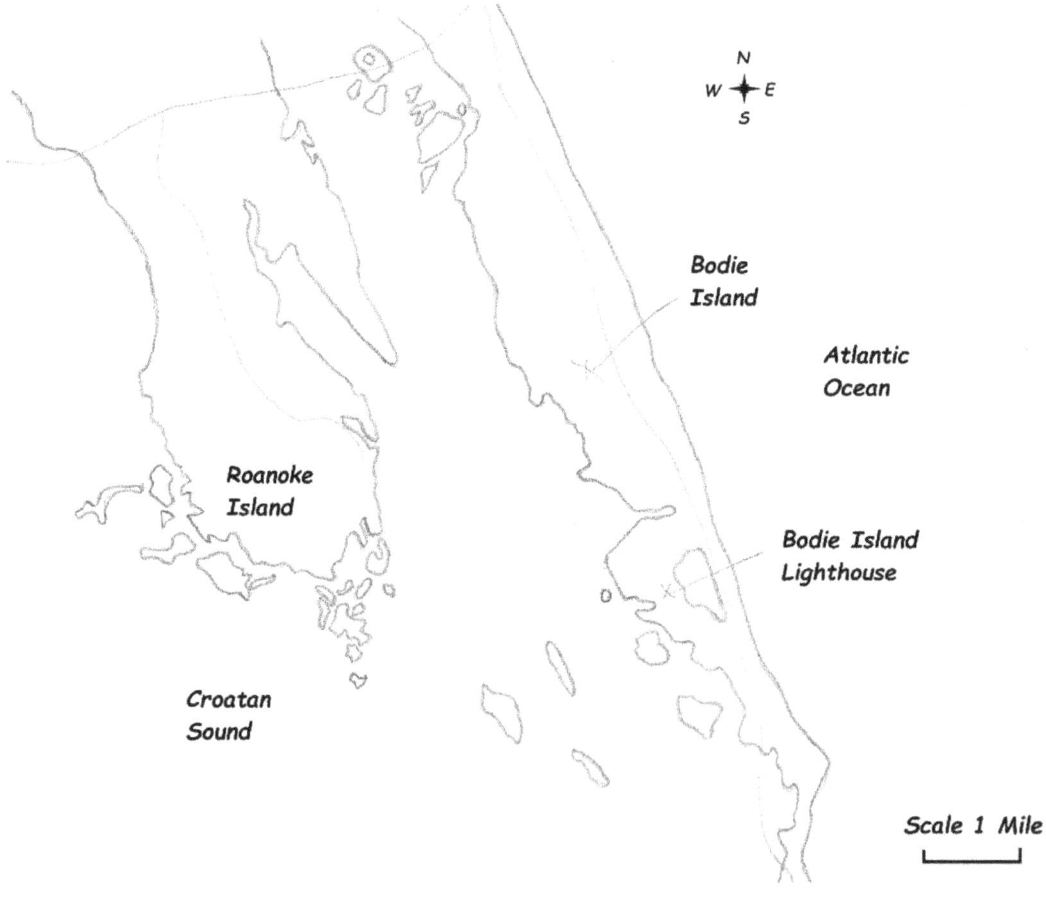

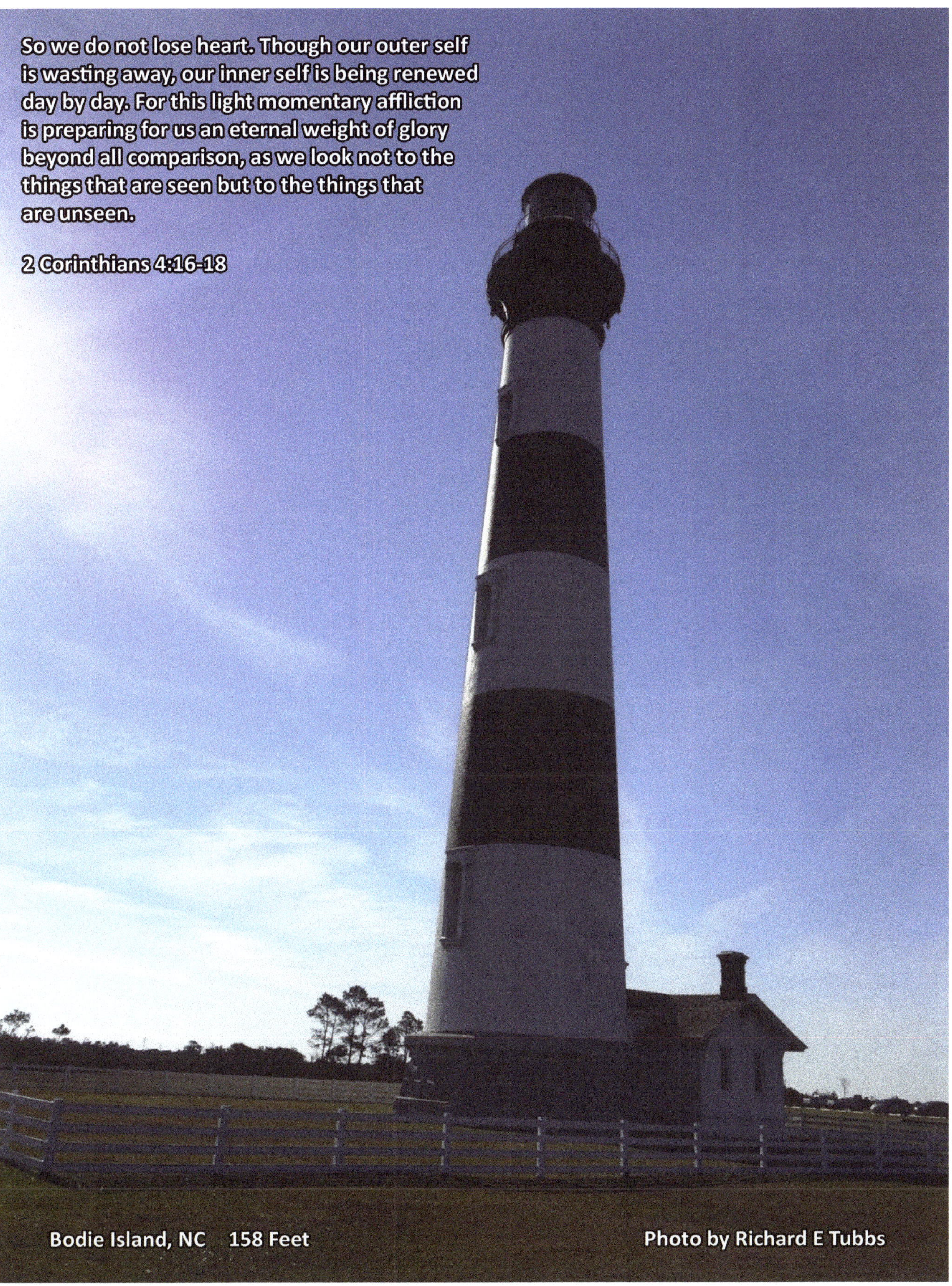

So we do not lose heart. Though our outer self is wasting away, our inner self is being renewed day by day. For this light momentary affliction is preparing for us an eternal weight of glory beyond all comparison, as we look not to the things that are seen but to the things that are unseen.

2 Corinthians 4:16-18

Bodie Island, NC   158 Feet

Photo by Richard E Tubbs

LOGGERHEAD KEY LIGHTHOUSE

LOGGERHEAD KEY LIGHTHOUSE, Dry Tortugas, Florida

Stands 157 feet tall. (1)

There are 203 granite block steps to the watch room. Restorations in the 1990's and early 2000's may have removed these and replaced them with iron staircase. Details are not readily available.

Built in 1858 on Loggerhead Key, three miles west of Garden Key and at the extreme western end of the Dry Tortugas islands.

Operated and maintained by the National Parks Service. Open to the public for day use only. Grounds are open year-round. All buildings and boat docks on Loggerhead Key are closed to the public. (2)

Uses a VRB-25 light. (3)

The light was converted to electric in 1931 by the use of generators. (4) And fully automated in 1982. (5)

The focal plane, how far out to sea it can be seen, is 19 nautical miles (6), depending on the size of your boat. The towers height and air clarity also determines how far out to sea it can be seen on any given night. (7)

Location: Loggerhead Key, three miles west of Garden Key, 70 miles west of Key West in the Dry Tortugas National Park (https://www.us-lighthouses.com/loggerhead-key-lighthouse).

But Jesus looked at them and said,
'With man this is impossible, but with
God all things are possible.'

Matthew 19:26

Loggerhead Key, FL   157 Feet

Photo by Richard E Tubbs

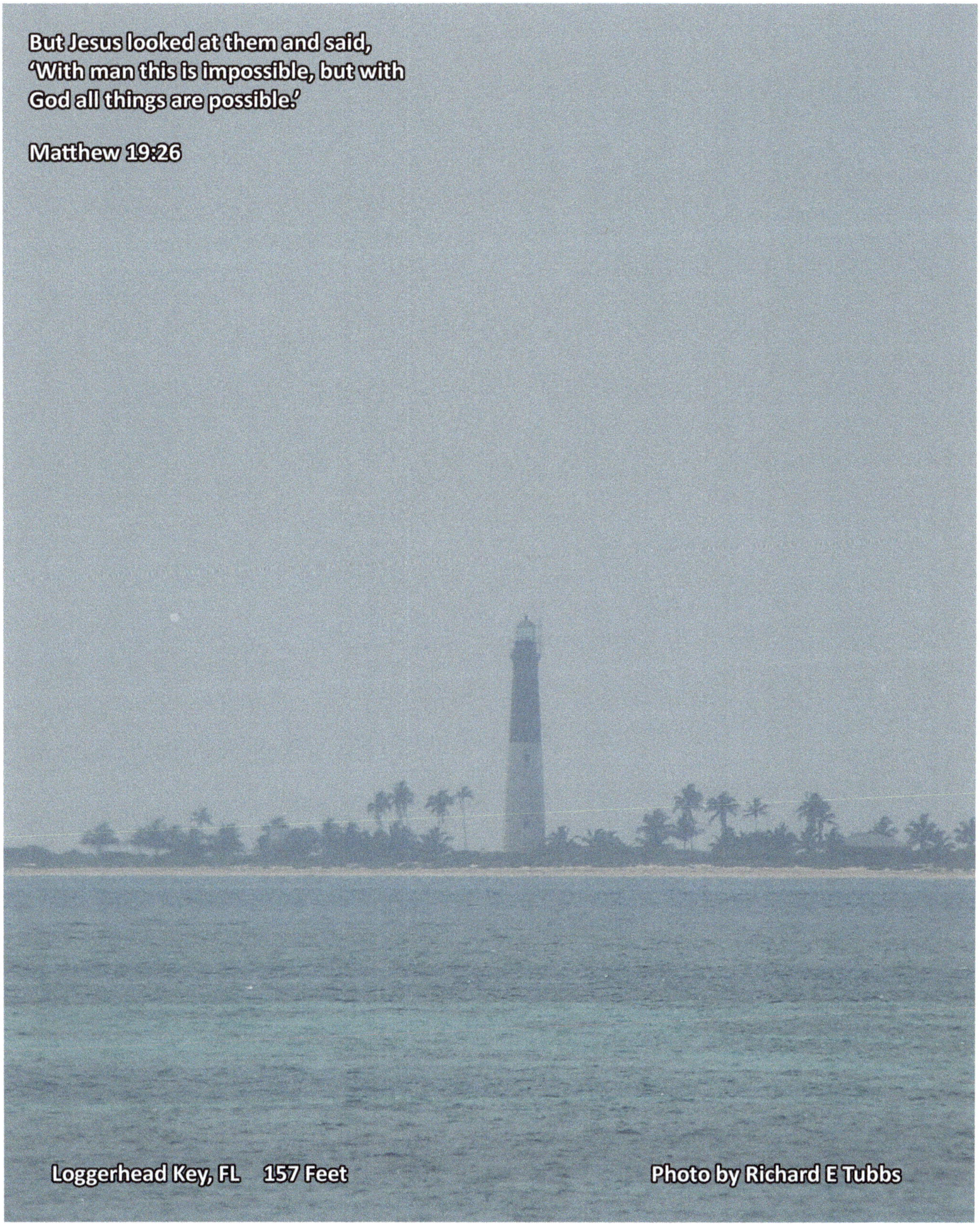

31

TYBEE ISLAND LIGHTHOUSE

TYBEE ISLAND LIGHTHOUSE, Tybee Island, Georgia

Stands 154 feet tall. (1)

There are 178 steps.

Built in 1867.

Operated by The Tybee Island Historical Society.

Open to the Public year-round but closed on Tuesdays. (2)

Fresnel Lens is 1st Order, the largest size, 12 feet tall and about 2,500 pounds of glass and bronze.

Present day beacon is electric, electrified in 1933 with a 30,000 candle-power light (3) from 1 1,000 watt bulb. With a second bulb ready to be automatically switched in when the first bulb burns out. (4) Automated in 1972. (5)

Focal plane, how far out to sea it can be seen, is 18 nautical miles (6), depending on the size of your boat. The towers height and air clarity, also, determines how far out to sea it can be seen on any given night. (7)

Location: On Tybee Island, Georgia, east of Savannah, Georgia. (8)

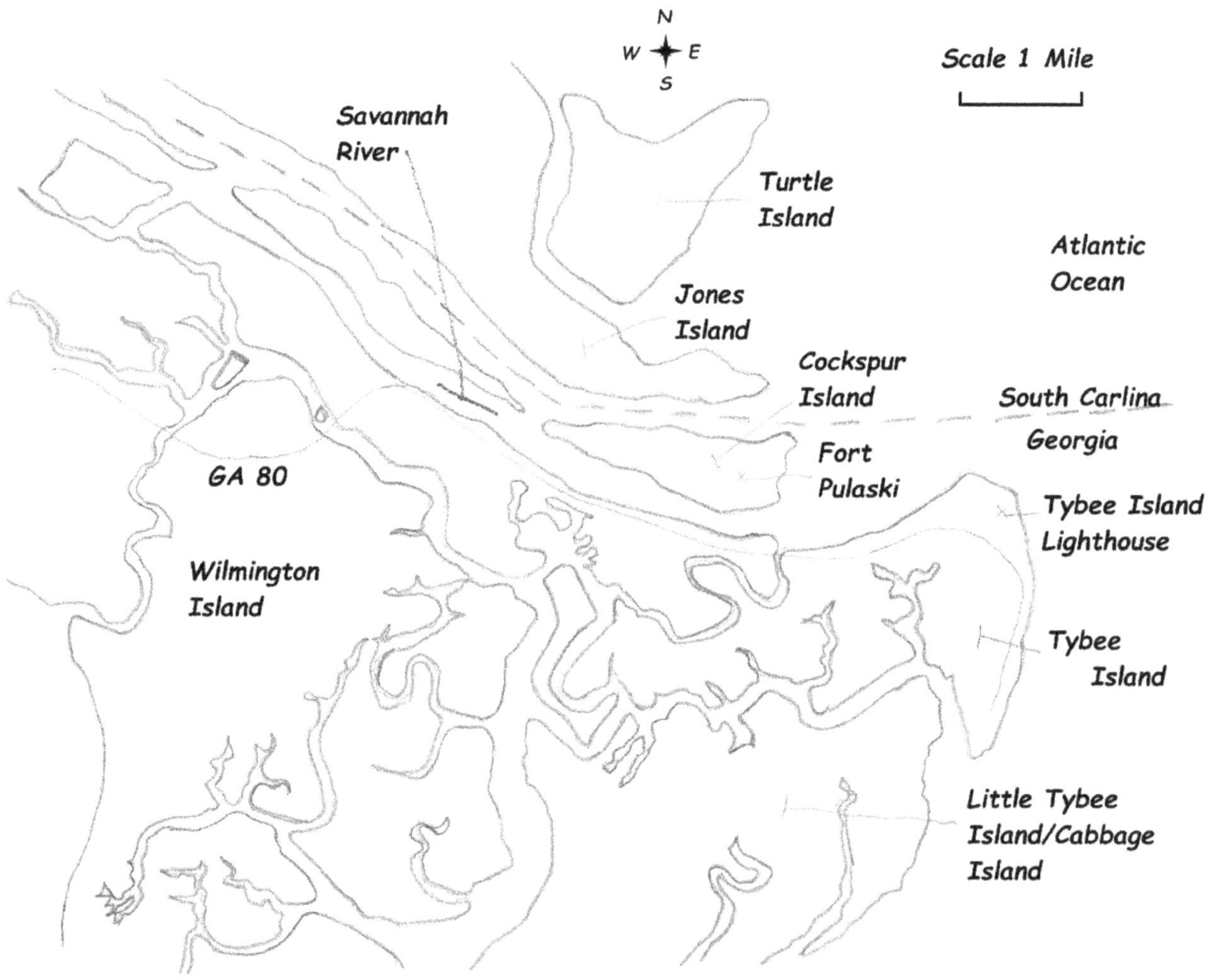

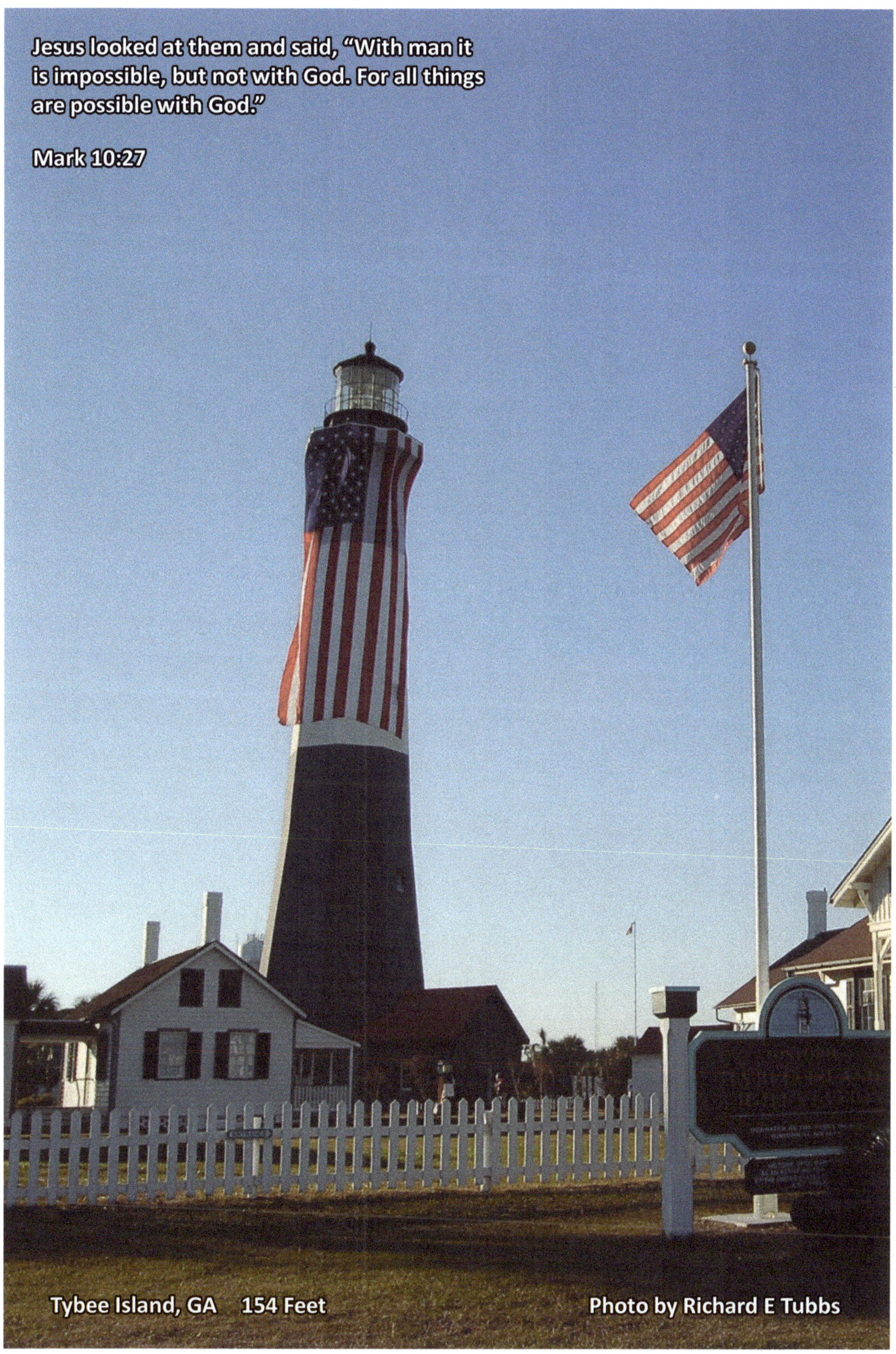
Jesus looked at them and said, "With man it
is impossible, but not with God. For all things
are possible with God."

Mark 10:27

Tybee Island, GA   154 Feet

Photo by Richard E Tubbs

OAK ISLAND LIGHTHOUSE

OAK ISLAND LIGHTHOUSE, Outer Banks, Caswell Beach, North Carolina

Stands 155 feet tall (1) Measured at 153 feet by the Friends of Oak Island Lighthouse.

There are 131 steps. (2)

Built in 1958.

Operated by the Town of Caswell Beach.

Open to the Public occasionally, (3) by appointment, tours are given by the Friends of Oak Island Lighthouse. (4)

Originally used a DCB-224 lens with 480 volt mercury arc lamps. Electrified since the day it was built. (5) Since the light itself is maintained by the Coast Guard, in December 2020, the light was upgraded to LED. (6)

Focal plane, how far out to sea it can be seen, is 18 nautical miles (7), depending on the size of your boat. The towers height and air clarity, also, determines how far out to sea it can be seen on any given night. (8)

Location: On Oak Island in Caswell Beach, North Carolina, the Southern section of the Outerbanks. (9)

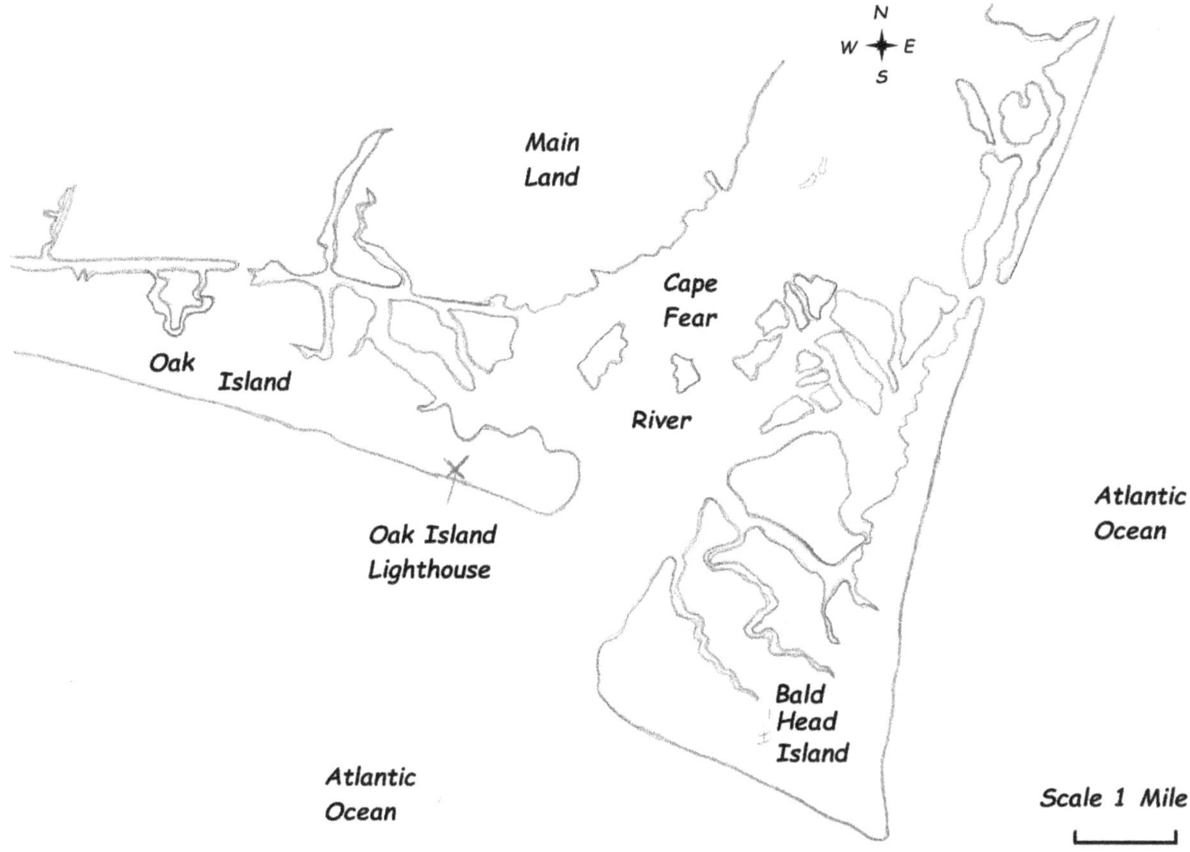

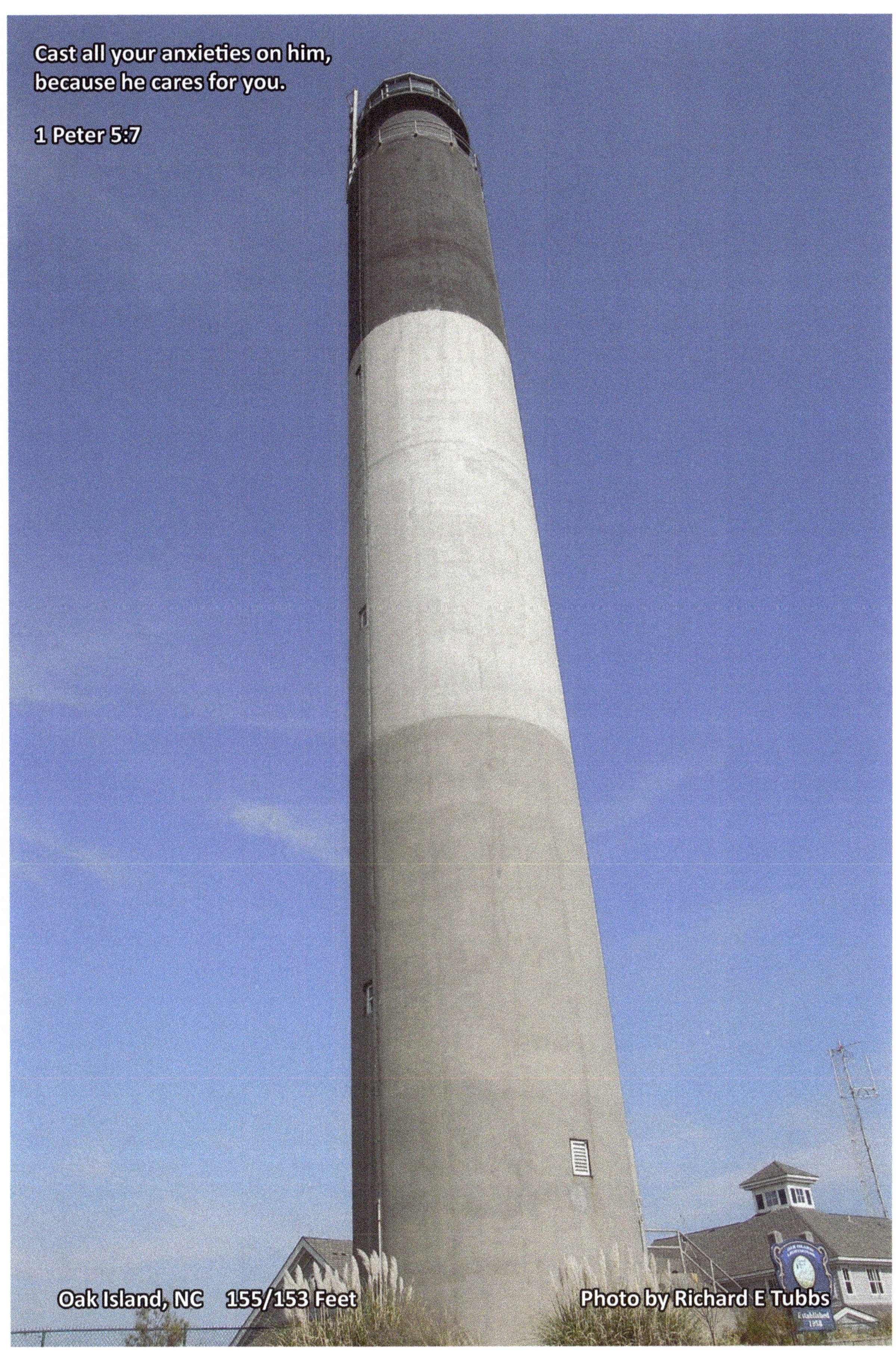
Cast all your anxieties on him,
because he cares for you.

1 Peter 5:7

Oak Island, NC   155/153 Feet

Photo by Richard E Tubbs

CAPE CANAVERAL
LIGHTHOUSE

CAPE CANAVERAL LIGHTHOUSE,
Cape Canaveral Space Force Station, Cape Canaveral, Florida

Stands 151 feet tall. (1)

There are 179 steps. (2)

Built in 1868.

Moved in 1893 to current site, 1.5 miles inland, old site is being taken back by the ocean.

Operated by the Cape Canaveral Lighthouse Foundation.

Since it is located on the Cape Canaveral Space Force Station, U.S. Space Force grounds, an active military site, it is only open to the public on Wednesdays by a guided tour year-round.

Originally equipped with a Fresnel Lens 1st Order, the largest size, 12 feet tall and about 2,500 pounds of glass and bronze. It currently has a DCB-224 rotating search light.

Present day beacon is electric, electrified in 1931. (3) Automated in 1967. It has two 1000-watt lamps with 800,000-candlepower rotary beacon, 2 flashes in 5 seconds followed by a 15 second eclipse. (4)

Focal plane, how far out to sea it can be seen, is 18 nautical miles (5), depending on the size of your boat. The towers height and air clarity, also, determines how far out to sea it can be seen on any given night. (6)

Location: On Cape Canaveral Air Force Station, Canaveral National Seashore, Cape Canaveral, Florida. (Location is derived from two websites, https://www.nps.gov/cana/index.htm and https://floridalighthouses.org/page-1106654 because the property/land is called Cape Canaveral with a specific area of that land called Canaveral National Seashore.)

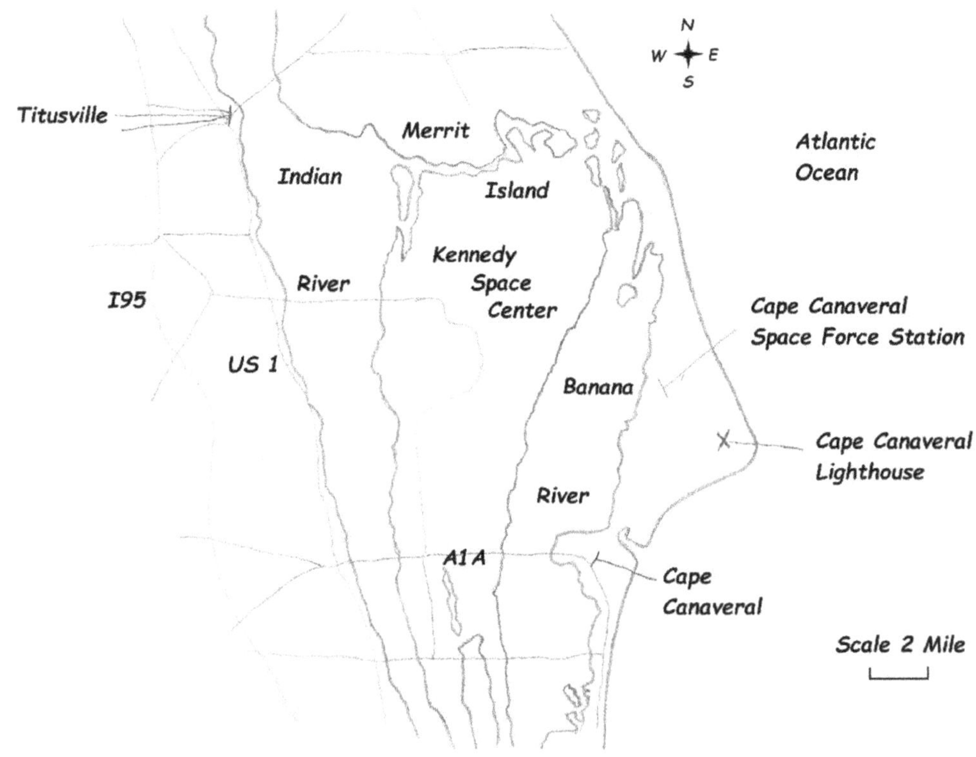

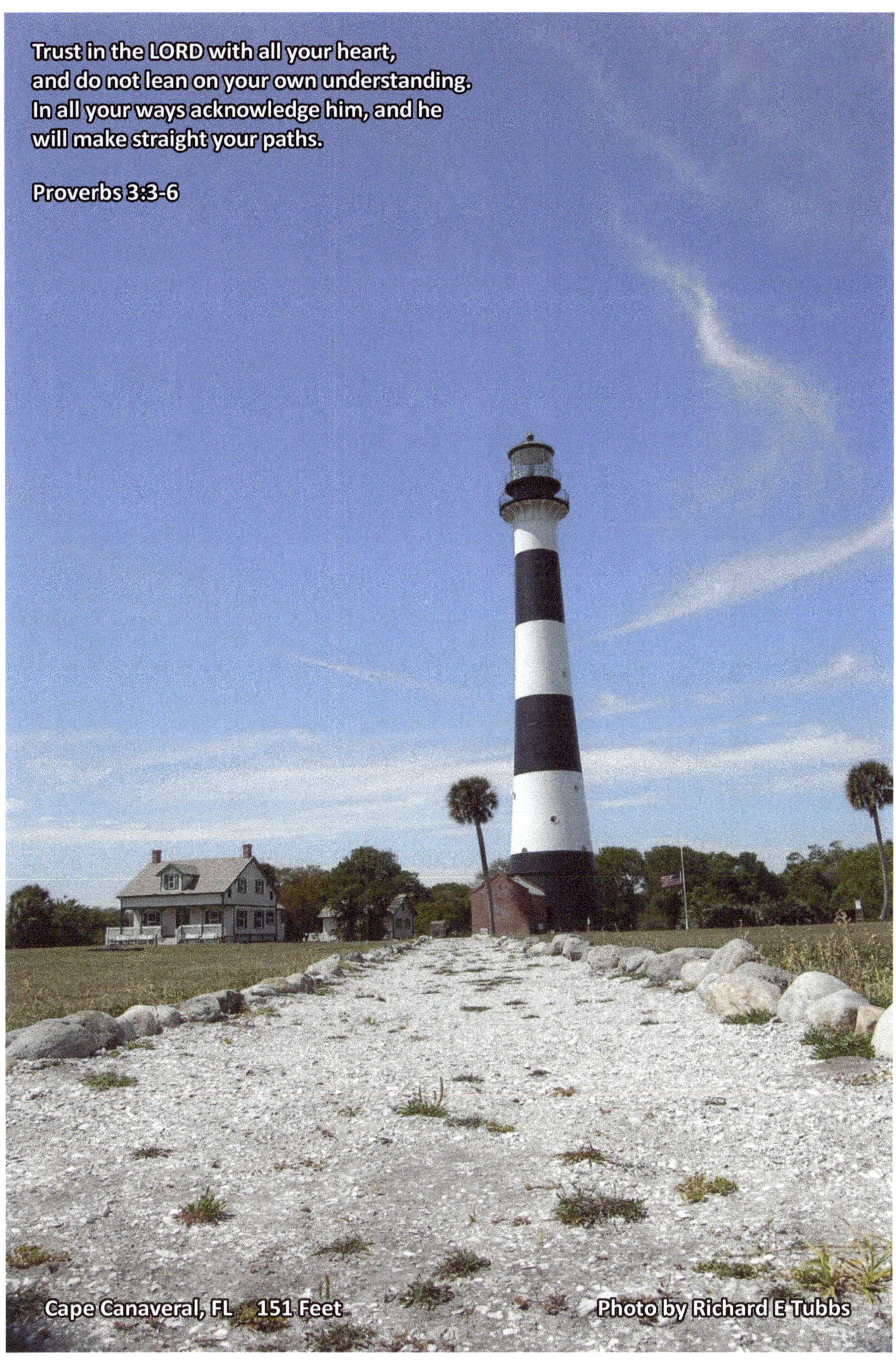

Trust in the LORD with all your heart,
and do not lean on your own understanding.
In all your ways acknowledge him, and he
will make straight your paths.

Proverbs 3:3-6

Cape Canaveral, FL   151 Feet
Photo by Richard E Tubbs

PENSACOLA LIGHTHOUSE

PENSACOLA LIGHTHOUSE,
Naval Air Station Pensacola, Pensacola, Florida

Stands 150 feet tall per Florida Lighthouse Association, Inc., 159 feet tall per (https://www.pensacolalighthouse.org/page/history) and some websites claiming 170+ feet tall.

There are 177 steps.

Built in 1858.

Operated by the Pensacola Lighthouse Association.

Since it is located on the Naval Air Station Pensacola, home to the Blue Angels, an active military site, visitors must use the Public Gate located at 1878 South Blue Angel Parkway. (The Navy Boulevard Gate is restricted to military personnel). The lighthouse and grounds are closed on Mondays, open all other days. As of November 7, 2022, civilians can only access the lighthouse by making a reservation and, then, ride in on the Lighthouses shuttlebus. (1)

Originally equipped with a Fresnel Lens 1st Order, the largest size, 12 feet tall and about 2,500 pounds of glass and bronze.

Present day beacon is electric, upgraded in 1939 and automated in 1965. The lighthouse currently uses four 1000-watt bulbs in the light, but only one is in operation at a time. When a bulb burns out, another automatically comes on. The powerful lens magnifies the light to 40,000 candlepower. With a white flash every 20 seconds. (2)

Focal plane, how far out to sea it can be seen, is 25 (3) to 27 (4) nautical miles, depending on the size of your boat. The towers height and air clarity, also, determines how far out to sea it can be seen on any given night. (5)

Location: On the grounds of the Naval Air Station Pensacola, Pensacola, Florida (6)

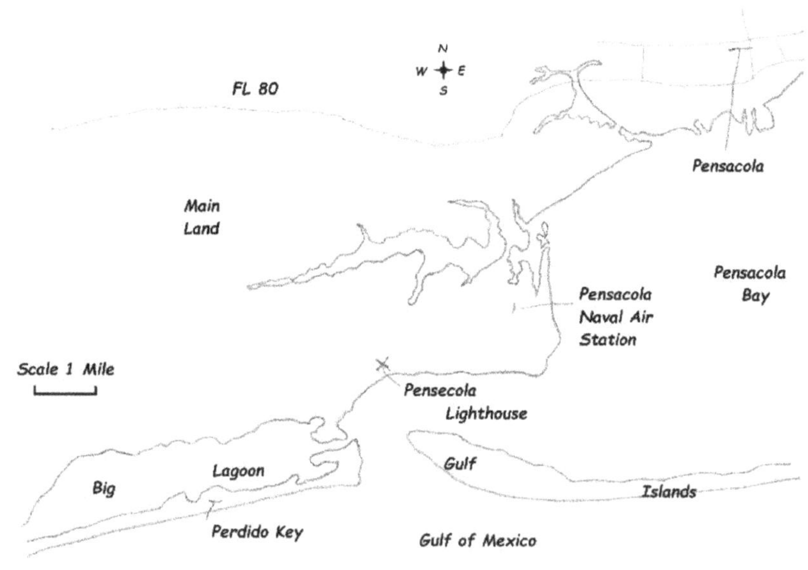

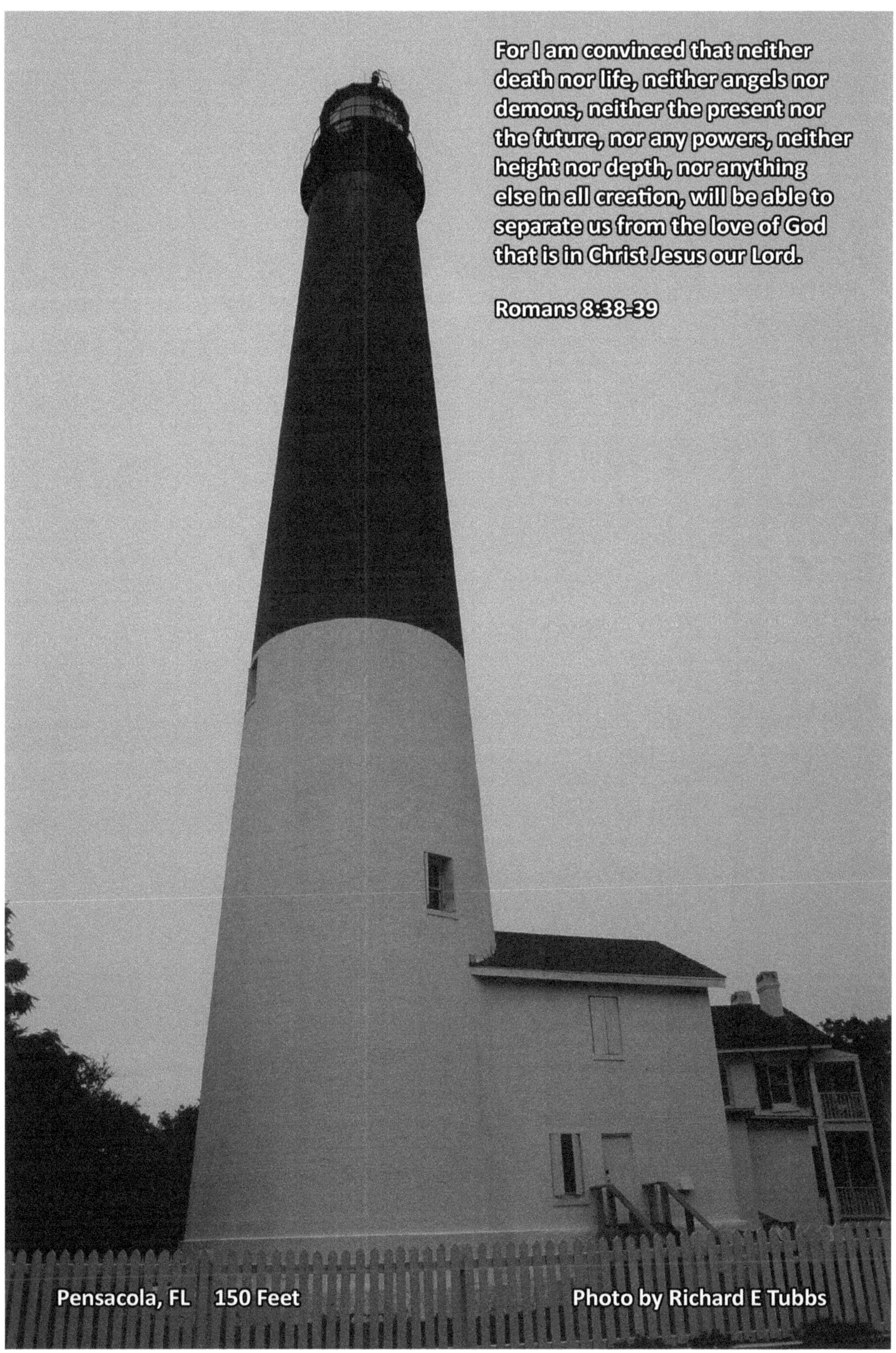
For I am convinced that neither death nor life, neither angels nor demons, neither the present nor the future, nor any powers, neither height nor depth, nor anything else in all creation, will be able to separate us from the love of God that is in Christ Jesus our Lord.

Romans 8:38-39

Pensacola, FL   150 Feet

Photo by Richard E Tubbs

Gratuitous meme, I climbed 203 Steps

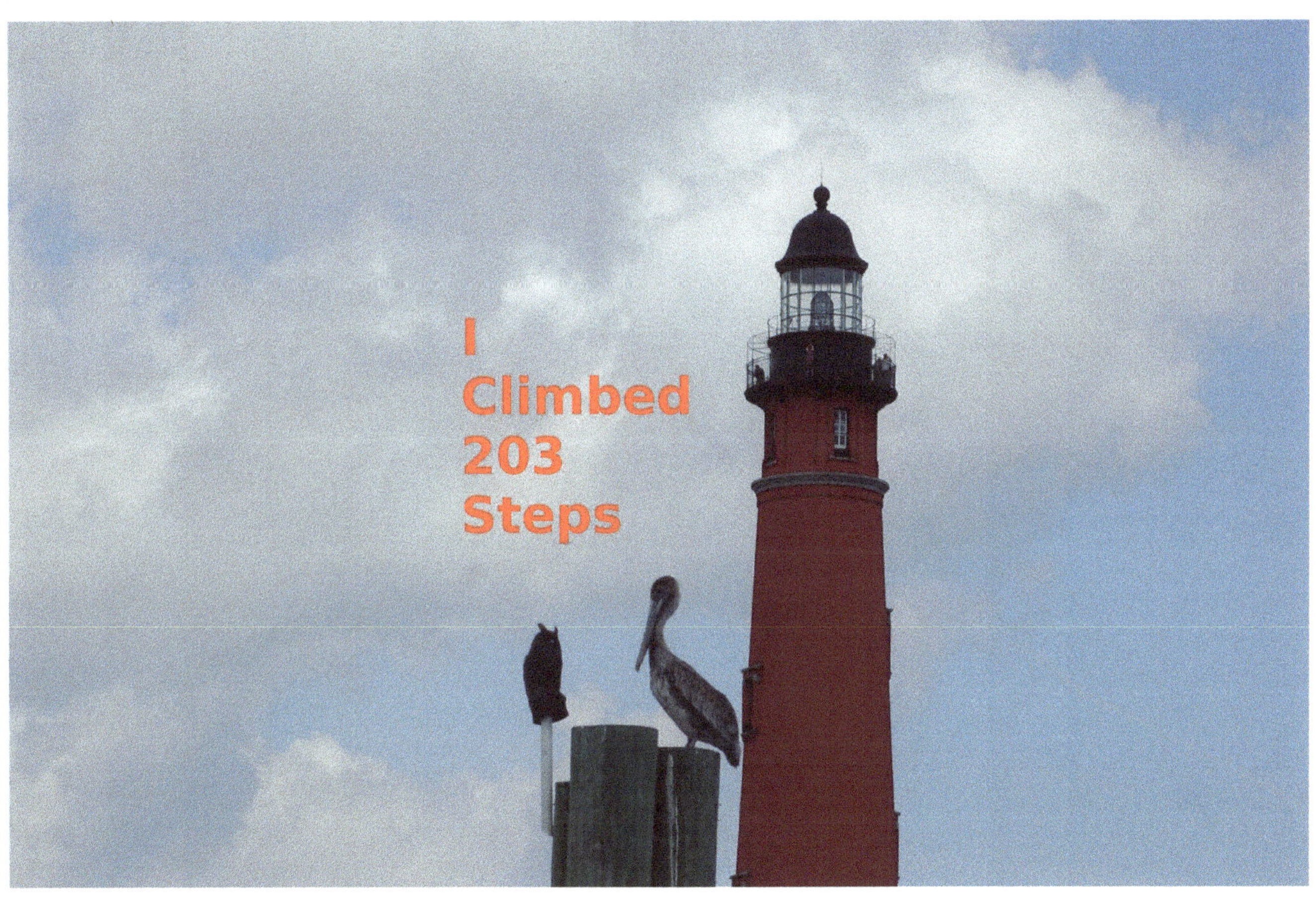

CONTROVERSIAL LIGHTHOUSES

Why include the Statue of Liberty and Perry Memorial as lighthouses? Because they are but not in the normal conventional sense. Which, is why many "purists" say they are not.

To summarize, many web pages and books etc, The Statue of Liberty is a lighthouse. You can start an in-depth research from these two sites: https://www.us-lighthouses.com/statue-of-liberty and https://web.archive.org/web/20170807205159/https://www.nps.gov/stli/faqs.htm.

It is a great day marker, as a beacon in the New York Skyline. But an awful nighttime aid to navigation. Its light cannot be seen very far or easily out to sea due to the design of the torch, that does not allow for a full 360 degree use. Many angles are blocked by the torch design so that light cannot be emitted out of the torch. The Statue of Liberty is best lit from external spotlights. This makes for a very shortrange navigation aid at night. It's original intent as a monument is how it works best.

The original torch was replaced in 1986. The new one had the flames covered in gold, making a nice reflective surface for daytime. The torch was then lit up at night with floodlights. So, it is easy to use for nighttime navigation from a few miles away. The address/location given for Lady Liberty is in New York Harbor, New York; but the same sources will also state that it is actually in New Jersey Waters – just go with it.

And this beacon should be on all lighthouse lovers bucket list to at least see, as I have done from a cruise ship.

Perry Memorial is also a lighthouse. It does not have any rotating light(s) but it does have four fixed lights on the top of each corner, plus the required aviation beacon lights.

On a clear day, you can see Canada (to the north) in the distance, 5 miles to be exact. The islands that Bass Island is part of are split, some to the North are Canadian and the rest are USA. Canadian mainland will be on the horizon to the north. You can also see Toledo (about 40 miles to the west). And to the east, the western suburbs of Cleveland.

Perry Memorial has been used as a maritime navigational aide since it was built in 1915. In July 1940, the Coast Guard noted in its bulletin that new lights had been added to the Perry Memorial, making the structure more beneficial for mariners.

This memorial is used as a maritime aid by international shippers, Canadian shippers, USA shippers, local shippers and by pleasure boaters of both Canada and the USA. The National Park Service owns and operates the light but you can find out more information at sites like these: https://www.us-light-houses.com/perrys-victory-memorial-lighthouse, https://www.lighthousefriends.com/light.asp?ID=277 and https://www.putinbay.org/attractions/perrys-victory-international-peace-memorial/.

With this being the 4th tallest memorial monument in the USA, making it one of the worlds tallest, you need to visit this one also.

STATUE OF LIBERTY

STATUE OF LIBERTY, Liberty Island, New York, New York

Also known as Lady Liberty. The official name is "The Statue of Liberty Enlightening the World". Dedicated as a national monument in 1924.

Height, base to top of torch is 151 feet, and from the ground to top of torch 305 feet.

There are 162 steps from the top of the pedestal to the crown that you can access. (1) There are 354 steps in all. (2)

Lady Liberty was a lighthouse from 1886 to 1902, and made a horrible one at that. Due to the design of the torch and in keeping the flame design, a light inside it appeared dim and badly lit as it was barely visible from nearby Manahatten Island. (3)

Construction started in 1875 and was completed in 1886.

The statue has been lit overnight since 1957. (4) Lady Liberty has had electricity since day one basically. First provided by generators and then by a dedicated line from the mainland of New York. (5) The torch observation deck has been closed since 1916 after German saboteurs tried to destroy it. (6)

Focal plane, how far out to sea it can be seen, when the torch was lit and from the right angle was 24 nautical miles (7), depending on the size of your boat. The towers height and air clarity, also, determines how far out to sea it can be seen on any given night. (8)

Location: Liberty Island, New York Harbor, New York, New York

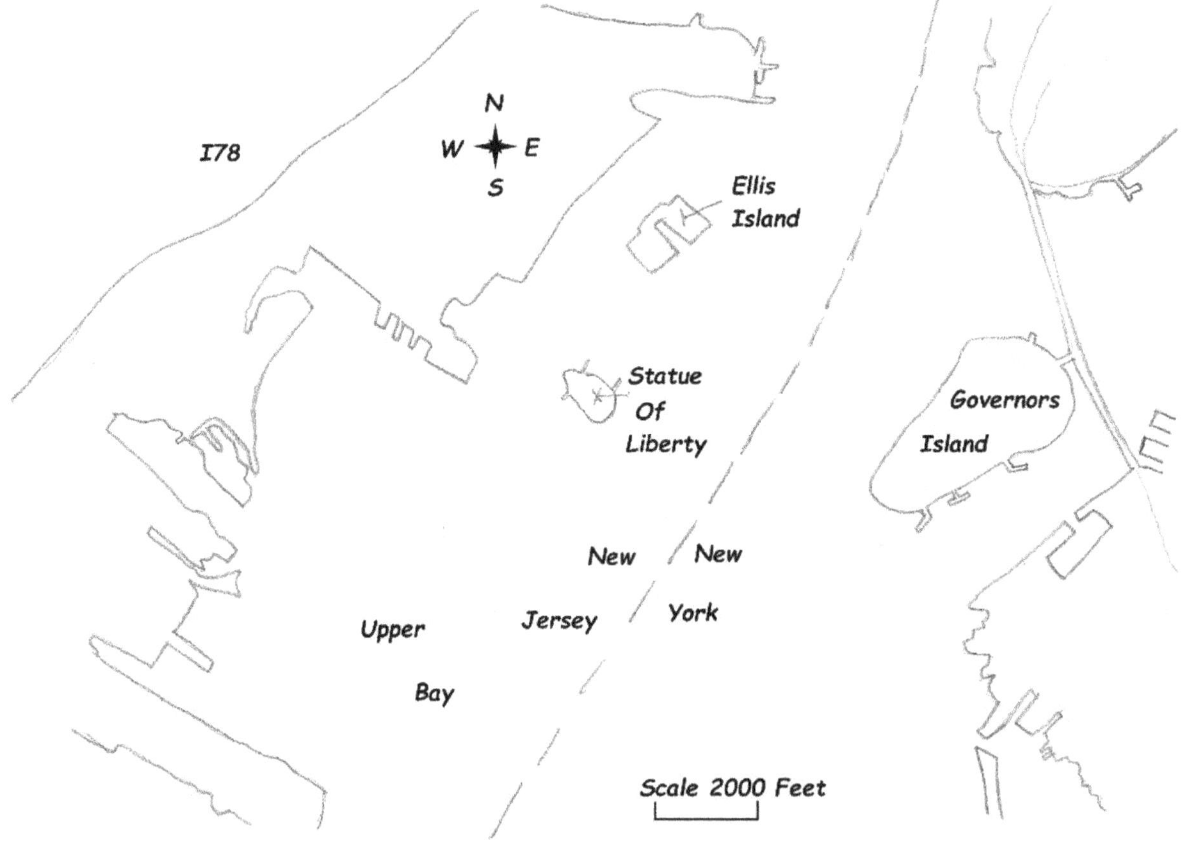

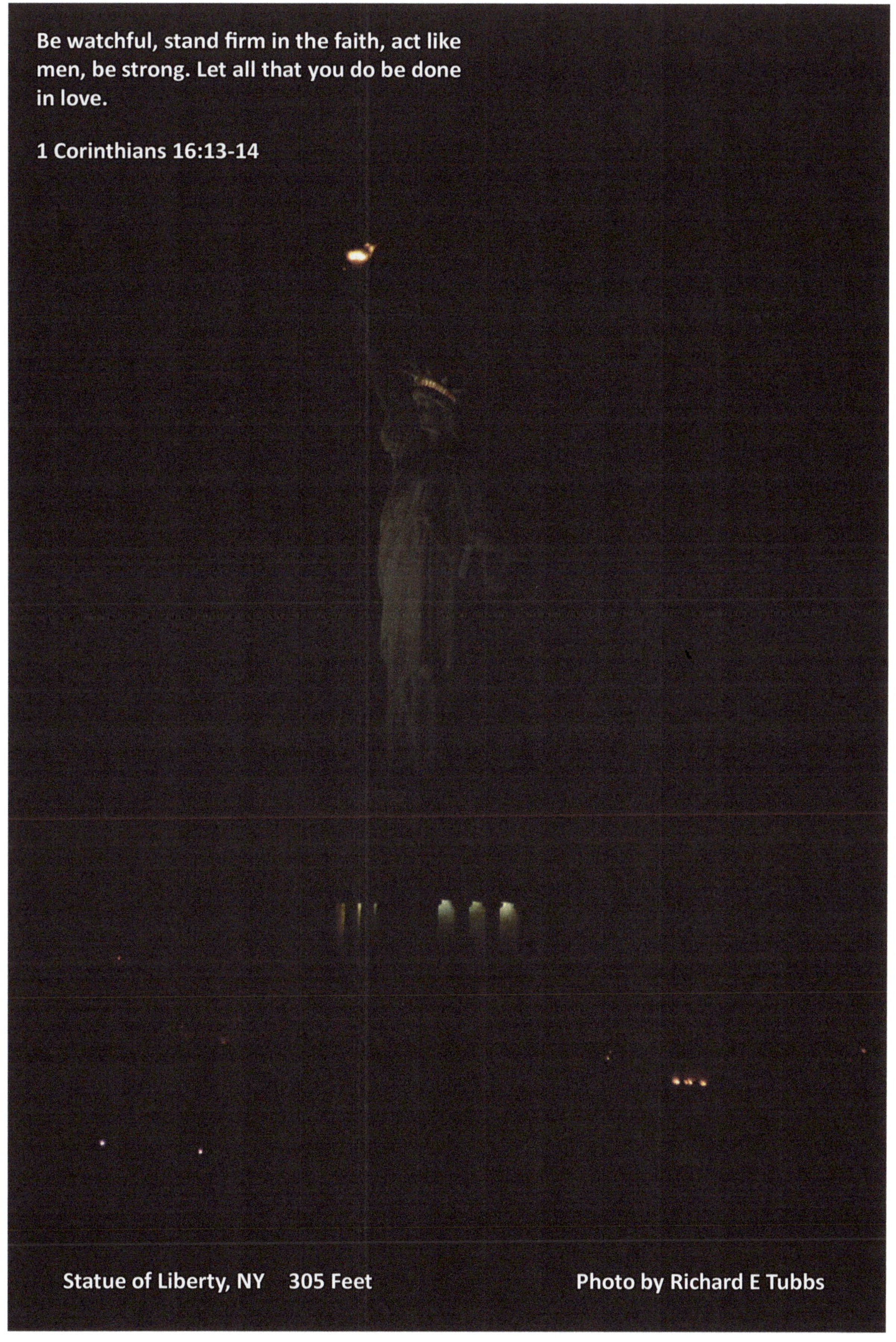

Statue of Liberty, NY   305 Feet   Photo by Richard E Tubbs

PERRY'S VICTORY AND INTERNATIONAL PEACE MEMORIAL

PERRY'S VICTORY AND INTERNATIONAL PEACE MEMORIAL,
Put-In-Bay, South Bass Island, Ohio

Stands 352 feet tall per the National Park Service. (1)

Steps, you can only climb the first 37 steps to the Lower Elevator Landing and then you have to take the elevator 317 feet to the top or upper elevator landing. (2) However, there are 427 steps from the Lower Elevator Landing to Upper Elevator Landing that are closed to the public. There are 3 Steps from the upper landing to observation deck. So, there are 40 steps to get to the top! (3)

Built in 1915. (4)

Owned by the National Park Service since 1936. The towers is open daily from mid-May through the first of October and the grounds are open year round. (5)

Officially Dedicated in 1931. And in 1936 declared a National Monument and transferred to the National Park Service. (6)

Electrified when built. No information is available on the type of lights used. It does not use a Fresnel Lens. It does use "marine type" lights as of April 5, 2021. (7)

The focal plane, how far out to sea it can be seen, is 40+ nautical miles and focal plane charts will say about 26 nautical miles (8), depending on the size of your boat. The towers height and air clarity, also, determines how far out to sea it can be seen on any given night. (9)

Location: Put-In-Bay, Isthmus on South Bass island, Ohio

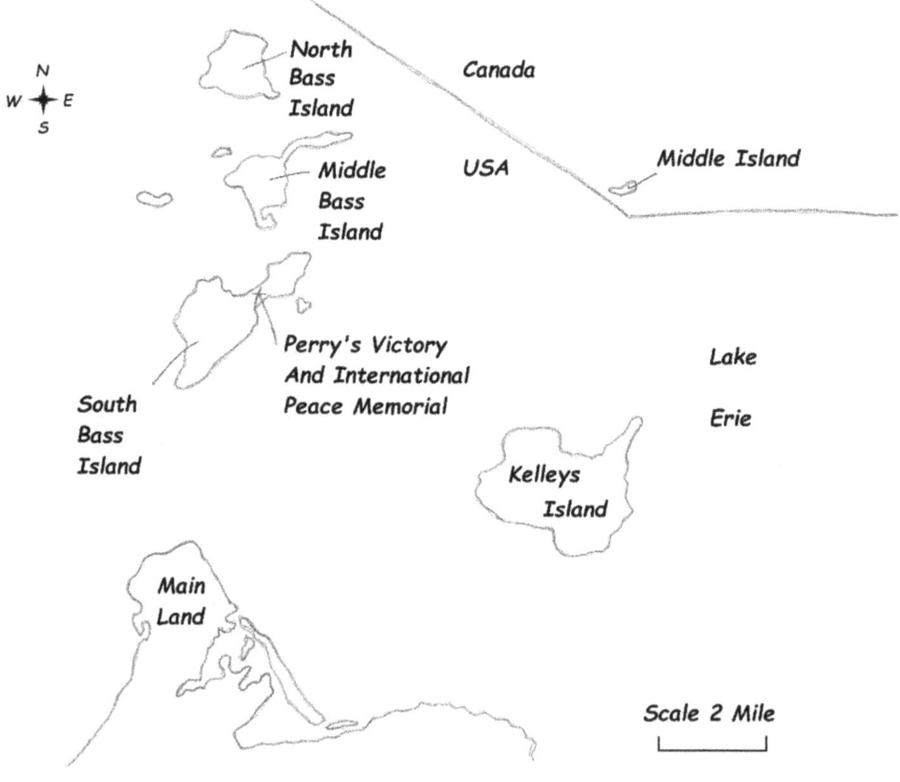

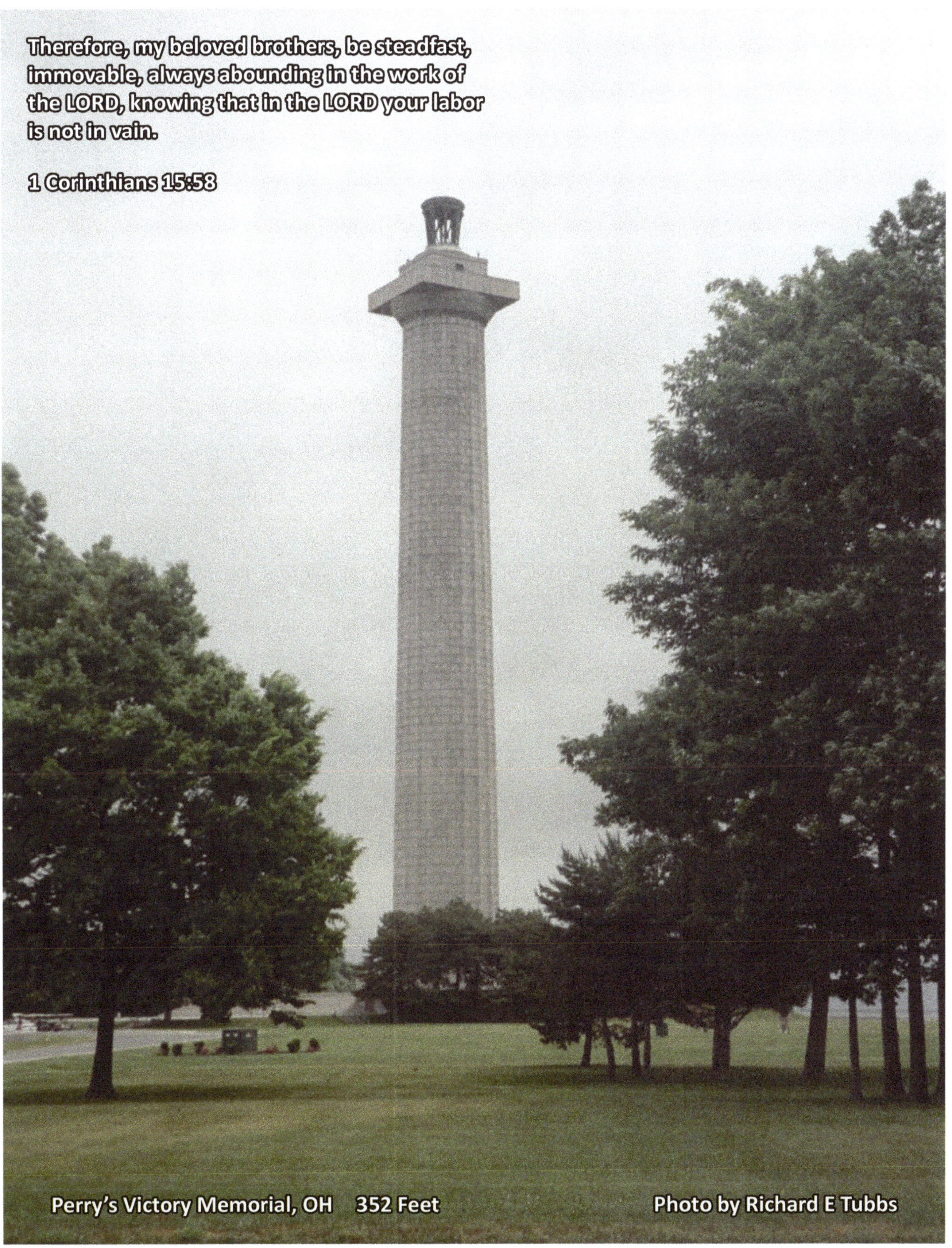
Therefore, my beloved brothers, be steadfast, immovable, always abounding in the work of the LORD, knowing that in the LORD your labor is not in vain.

1 Corinthians 15:58

Perry's Victory Memorial, OH   352 Feet

Photo by Richard E Tubbs

Checklist for Lighthouses you have visited.

Cape Hatteras		Ponce de Leon Inlet		St Augustine		Cape Lookout		Currituck Beach	
Morris Island		Bodie Island		Loggerhead Key		Tybee Island		Oak Island	
Cape Canaveral		Pensacola		Statue of Liberty		Perry's Victory and International Peace Memorial			

CREDITS / BIBLIOGRAPHY

Cape Hatteras

1, 4 – https://www.outerbanks.com/cape-hatteras-lighthouse.html
2, 3, 5, 7 – https://www.nps.gov/caha/planyourvisit/chls.htm
6 – https://www.uscg.mil/Portals/0/OurOrganization/auxiliary/publications/auxmanuals/
ATON2000StudyGuideSec2ATON.pdf?ver=2017-07-02-093515-290

Ponce de Leon Inlet

1, 3, 5 – https://www.ponceinlet.org/
2, 4 – https://www.uscg.mil/Portals/0/OurOrganization/auxiliary/publications/auxmanuals/
ATON2000StudyGuideSec2ATON.pdf?ver=2017-07-02-093515-290

St Augustine

1, 4, 6 – https://www.staugustinelighthouse.org/2019/04/30/%EF%BB%BFfrequently-asked-ques-
tions-by-lighthouse-visitors/
2 – https://web.archive.org/web/20170501202325/http://www.uscg.mil/history/weblighthouses/LHFL.asp
3 – https://www.florida-backroads-travel.com/st-augustine-lighthouse.html
5 – https://www.uscg.mil/Portals/0/OurOrganization/auxiliary/publications/auxmanuals/
ATON2000StudyGuideSec2ATON.pdf?ver=2017-07-02-093515-290

Cape Lookout

1, 3, 7 – https://www.nps.gov/calo/index.htm
2 – https://web.archive.org/web/20160904022527/http://www.carolinalights.com/
north-carolina-lighthouses/cape-lookout-lighthouse
4 – https://www.bpr.org/news/2017-05-09/cape-lookout-lighthouse-switches-to-solar
5 – https://www.outerbanks.com/cape-lookout-lighthouse.html
6 – https://www.uscg.mil/Portals/0/OurOrganization/auxiliary/publications/auxmanuals/
ATON2000StudyGuideSec2ATON.pdf?ver=2017-07-02-093515-290

Currituck Beach

1, 3 – https://obcinc.org/visit-our-sites/currituck-beach-lighthouse/

2 – https://www.us-lighthouses.com/currituck-beach-lighthouse

4 – https://www.uscg.mil/Portals/0/OurOrganization/auxiliary/publications/auxmanuals/ATON2000StudyGuideSec2ATON.pdf?ver=2017-07-02-093515-290

5 – https://www.us-lighthouses.com/currituck-beach-lighthouse

Morris Island

1 – https://www.visit-historic-charleston.com/morris-island-lighthouse.html

2, 5 – https://www.follybeach.com/lighthouse/

3 – https://www.us-lighthouses.com/morris-island-lighthouse

4, 7 – https://www.uscg.mil/Portals/0/OurOrganization/auxiliary/publications/auxmanuals/ATON2000StudyGuideSec2ATON.pdf?ver=2017-07-02-093515-290

6 – http://www.nationalregister.sc.gov/charleston/S10817710119/S10817710119.pdf

8 – https://savethelight.org/

Bodie Island

1, 3, 5, 7 – https://www.outerbanks.com/bodie-island-lighthouse.html

2, 4 – https://www.nps.gov/caha/planyourvisit/bils.htm

6 – (https://www.uscg.mil/Portals/0/OurOrganization/auxiliary/publications/auxmanuals/ATON2000StudyGuideSec2ATON.pdf?ver=2017-07-02-093515-290

Loggerhead Key

1, 3 – https://www.us-lighthouses.com/loggerhead-key-lighthouse

2, 4, 6 – https://www.nps.gov/drto/planyourvisit/loggerhead-key.htm

5 – https://www.nps.gov/drto/learn/historyculture/lighthouses.htm

7 – https://www.uscg.mil/Portals/0/OurOrganization/auxiliary/publications/auxmanuals/ATON2000StudyGuideSec2ATON.pdf?ver=2017-07-02-093515-290

Tybee Island

1, 5 – http://www.lighthousedigest.net/Digest/database/uniquelighthouse.cfm?value=398

2, 4, 8 – https://www.tybeelighthouse.org/general-1-1

3, 6 – https://www.savannah.com/tybee-island-lighthouse/

7 – https://www.uscg.mil/Portals/0/OurOrganization/auxiliary/publications/auxmanuals/ATON2000StudyGuideSec2ATON.pdf?ver=2017-07-02-093515-290

Oak Island

1, 3, 5 – http://www.lighthousedigest.net/Digest/database/uniquelighthouse.cfm?value=882

2, 4, 6, 9 – http://www.oakislandlighthouse.org/

7 – https://us-lighthouses.com/tybee-island-lighthouse

8 – https://www.uscg.mil/Portals/0/OurOrganization/auxiliary/publications/auxmanuals/ATON2000StudyGuideSec2ATON.pdf?ver=2017-07-02-093515-290

Cape Canaveral

1, 3, 5 – https://canaverallight.org/

2, 4 – https://floridalighthouses.org/page-1106654

6 – https://www.uscg.mil/Portals/0/OurOrganization/auxiliary/publications/auxmanuals/ATON2000StudyGuideSec2ATON.pdf?ver=2017-07-02-093515-290

Pensacola

1, 6 – https://www.pensacolalighthouse.org/

2 – https://floridalighthouses.org/page-1106685

3 – http://www.lighthouseinn-ct.com/lighthouses-by-state/florida-lighthouses/pensacola-lighthouse.html

4 – https://www.ycaol.com/light29.htm

5 https://www.uscg.mil/Portals/0/OurOrganization/auxiliary/publications/auxmanuals/ATON2000StudyGuideSec2ATON.pdf?ver=2017-07-02-093515-290

Statue of Liberty

1 – https://www.nps.gov/stli/index.htm

2 – https://www.answers.com/Q/How_many_stairs_are_there_in_the_Statue_of_Liberty

3, 6 – https://www.worldatlas.com/articles/10-amazing-facts-about-the-statue-of-liberty.html

3, 5 – https://www.us-lighthouses.com/statue-of-liberty

7 – https://www.lighthousedigest.com/Digest/database/uniquelighthouse.cfm?value=780

8 – https://www.uscg.mil/Portals/0/OurOrganization/auxiliary/publications/auxmanuals/ATON2000StudyGuideSec2ATON.pdf?ver=2017-07-02-093515-290

Perry Memorial

1 – https://www.nps.gov/places/perry-s-victory.htm?utm_source=place&utm_medium=website&utm_campaign=experience_more&utm_content=small

2, 5 – https://www.nps.gov/pevi/planyourvisit/basicinfo.htm

3, 8 – Email from Whitman, Robert O <Robert_Whitman@nps.gov>

4 – https://www.youtube.com/watch?v=B9BV6v-VSCs&feature=youtu.be

6, 7 – https://www.lighthousefriends.com/light.asp?ID=277

9 – https://www.uscg.mil/Portals/0/OurOrganization/auxiliary/publications/auxmanuals/ATON2000StudyGuideSec2ATON.pdf?ver=2017-07-02-093515-290